MW00479000

Ethiopia

THE LOST KINGDOM-SAVING CHRISTIANITY
THE UNTOLD STORY

A Future New York Times Bestseller

Dr. Lawrence E. Henry Ed.D

(Licensed Psychologist)

ISBN 978-1-0980-4110-6 (paperback)
ISBN 978-1-0980-4111-3 (digital)

Copyright © 2020 by Dr. Lawrence E. Henry Ed.D

All rights reserved. No part of this publication may be reproduced, distributed, or transmitted in any form or by any means, including photocopying, recording, or other electronic or mechanical methods without the prior written permission of the publisher. For permission requests, solicit the publisher via the address below.

Christian Faith Publishing, Inc.
832 Park Avenue
Meadville, PA 16335
www.christianfaithpublishing.com

Printed in the United States of America

To my best friend, Kum (Sony), for being a godly, gorgeous, excellent wife and mother. Our favorite verse: "Truly, truly, I say to you, if anyone keeps my word, he will never see death" (John 8:51).

This book is dedicated to those who will accept and appreciate the truth. Let the light shine through.

[In 650 BC,] Word reached
the Assyrian Army, that the
Egyptian army, led by King
Tirhakah of Ethiopia, was
coming to attack them.
—2 Kings 19:9
(*In defense of Jerusalem*)

Soon afterward King Sennacherib
received word that King Tirhakah of
Ethiopia was leading an army to fight
against him. Before leaving to meet
the attack, he sent messengers back to
Hezekiah in Jerusalem with this message.
—Isaiah 37:9

Contents

Introduction

My first book, *In Search of Wisdom: The Pickle Jar Theory*, after being released in October 2008, is being offered in over 150 different countries and 250 internet sites. It contained a treasure of information concerning scientific wisdom revealed by God. *In Search of Wisdom: The Pickle Jar Theory* was described as a book that combines ancient wisdom and the science of today and melds both in a way that makes perfect sense. More than making sense, science of today is embracing and looking back at the scientific wisdom of the Bible, realizing that it holds true today.

My second book, *Fruit of the Spirit: Biblical Psychology*, was a continuation of wisdom revealed in the Bible as it relates to the psychology of the mind, physical health, and mental status. God warns us about ways of life that threaten our health and happiness.

Fruit of the Spirit: Biblical Psychology contained wisdom from a psychological perpective to prolong our life and improve health. This book will show how the Bible is the operations manual to obtain a healthy long life physically and mentally.

My Korean pastor, Junghee Yoon, gave a sermon on discrimination and how sinful God perceived judging people on skin color. He referenced the book of Numbers 12:1–10. God's reaction to Miriam and Aaron's behavior toward

Moses's Ethiopian wife were very severe. That sermon motivated me to research other Ethiopians in the Bible.

The foundation of my interest in Africa began at the age of five with my grandfather talking about his father (slave) and their strong relationship with the Lord. As early as five years old, my grandfather lectured me on my resemblance to Jesus and that Jesus was inside of me.

Shortly after the sermon concerning Moses and his Ethiopian wife, I read another story in Acts 8:26–39 about an Ethiopian official and the apostle Phillip. This story gives an example of God's intentions to spread Christianity to the world and how he specifically used Ethiopians for this purpose. The story in Acts will be covered in part 3 of this book.

The baptism of the Ethiopian official in the book of Acts was very significant to the spread of Christianity to the world, although no minster had ever included it in a sermon that I could recall. In fact, the biblical stories concerning Ethiopia has been ignored in the religious community.

In numerous verses in the Bible, Ethiopia is referenced and relevant to the spread of Christianity. *It would be hard to overstate the impact of Ethiopia and the Ethiopian people on the advancement of Christianity.*

In chapter 8, we will fast-forward two thousand years and find the Ethiopian Church has a membership of between 40 and 46 million; Christians which make up about 60 percent of the total population of the country. Ethiopia was also the first country to declare Christianity a state religion and has never been occupied by a foreign country.

The study of the Bible and other ancient writings tell the full story of Ethiopia! This book will explain how God commissioned the Ethiopians to work for the kingdom of God and to spread Christianity geographically and ethically to the ends of the earth.

What was discovered in the Bible concerning Ethiopia was prodigiously incredible. *Thoughout the old and new testament the Israels did evil in the eyes of the Lord by serving other Gods, sinning and violating the covenant. The Lords anger, burned against the Israelis during these times.*

The relationship among God, Ethiopia, and the Ethiopian people represents the "greatest story never told" until now. Ethiopia's place in God's story is truly profound as you will see in this book.

Writing this book was a very difficult task; I relied on the Lord and his wisdom. Often Philippians 1:6 is referred to during the writing of this book, and I must constantly keep in mind "being confident of this that he who began a good work in you will carry it on to completion until the day of Christ Jesus." This book represents a story that needed to be told and God-inspired.

Chapter 1

Bibiblical Scriptures Relating to Ethiopia

A Message to Cush (Ethiopia)

This book is full of scriptures relating to Ethiopia and is a systemic examination of the prophesizes and instructions to Ethiopia. These verses show how God used Ethiopia to ensure the continuation of the Jewish people, supporting the kingdom of heaven.

There are many prophecies and signs specifically referenced to Ethiopia and the Ethiopian people. These signs and prophecies were given to build faith and point to his Son.

In many of these verses, Ethiopian accepted Jesus and the God of Abraham as their Savior and qualified as children of God as stipulated in the book of Galatians.

> So in Christ Jesus you are all children of God through faith, for all of you who were baptized into Christ have clothed yourselves with Christ. There is neither Jew nor Gentile, neither slave nor free, nor is there male and female, for you

are all one in Christ Jesus. If you belong
to Christ, then you are Abraham's seed,
and heirs according to the promise."
(Gal. 3:26–29)

In fact, God clarified his declaration in the book of
Amos.

Are ye not as children of the
Ethiopians unto me, O children of Israel?
saith the Lord. Have not I brought up
Israel out of the land of Egypt? and the
Philistines from Caphtor, and the Syrians
from Kir. (Amos 9:7)

The following verses below concerning Ethiopia are
very relevant, listing how Ethiopia was used, showing instructions and tasks assigned exclusively to Ethiopia. Each of these
verses will be covered separately in this book.

- *Foreigners* come from a distant land because of your
  name (1 Kings 8:41–43).
- *Queen of Sheba* visits Solomon (Isa. 10:1–13).
- Word reaching the Assyrians from King Tirhakah
  (*Ethiopian King* in charge of the Egyptian army),
  causing the defeat of the Assyrians (Isa. 39:9 and 2
  Kings 19:9).
- The *Queen of Sheba* visits Solomon (2 Chron.
  9:1–12).
- A prophecy against *Cush* (*Ethiopia*) (Isa. 18:1–7).
- Princes shall come out of Egypt. *Ethiopia* shall
  stretch out her hands unto God (Ps. 68:31).

- The kings of Sheba and Seba present him gifts (Ps. 72:10).
- An oracle concerning *Cush/Ethiopia*—trumpet sound, banner raised, and gifts to the God (Isa. 18:1–7).
- Gifts to the Lord of Host in Zion from the Ethiopians (Isa. 18:7).
- The glory of Zion and all from Sheba will come, bearing gold and incense and proclaiming the praise of the Lord (Isa. 60:1–17).
- *Ebedmelech the Ethiopian* saves Jeremiah (Jer. 38:7–13).
- God saves Ebed-Melech from those plotting to kill him (Jer. 39:15–18).
- The Lord comparing *Ethiopians* and children of Israel both as his children (Amos 9:7).
- *Ethiopians* bringing offerings/gifts to the Lord (Zeph. 3:10).
- The *Queen of the South* will condemn this generation. She came to listen to Solomon's wisdom, and now someone greater than Solomon is here [A miracle demonstrated by God] (Matt. 12:42).
- The sign of Jonah—*the Queen of the South* will rise at judgment (Luke 11:29–32).
- Apostle Phillip baptizes the Ethiopian (Acts 8:26–29).

It maybe a surprise to know that in the Bible, only Israel surpasses the total number of instructions and verses toward any nation other than Ethiopia. Most of the bibilical writings concerning Israel reflect on how they sinned and the miracles performed by God to support and carry out the promises he had made with them.

As mentioned in the introduction, "Throughout the Old and New Testaments, the Israelites did evil in the eyes of the Lord by serving other gods, sinning and violating the covenant. The Lords anger burned against the Israelites during these times."

In contrast, most of the instructions concerning Ethiopia consist of actions to benefit the kingdom of heaven. Down through history, God provided Ethiopia a road map and foretold various signs and conditions through his prophets all for the kingdom of heaven. These prophets spoke of things that mankind should watch for so that the Messiah would be recognized and believed.

The Old Testament written hundreds of years before Jesus's birth contains over 250 prophecies that Jesus fulfilled through his life, death, and resurrection.

Chapter 2

Miriam and Aaron Criticize Moses's Ethiopian (Cushite) Wife

And he said to Moses, "Please, my Lord,
I ask you not to hold against us the
sin we have so foolishly committed."
—Numbers 12:11

That sin was critizing an Ethiopian woman! Apparently, that woman was the wife God had chosen for Moses. The first clue as to how special Ethiopians were is revealed in Numbers 12. God was not happy with the treatment of Moses's Ethiopian wife and admitted that it was a grave sin. God pointed out the importance of Moses and that he was the only prophet that he appeared in person mouth to mouth and not in a vision like the other prophets.

Other than Moses and probably Abraham, God never appeared face-to-face (mouth to mouth in God's words) to any other person. Moses's Ethiopian wife was also considered very, very special to have been chosen for Moses's wife.

The marriage would never have happened without God's approval.

God found it necessary and important enough to meet Aaron and Miriam at the door of the tabernacle to discuss the rejection of the Ethiopian. God's selection of the Ethiopian wife for Moses was for a reason only God knew!

There are conflicting opinions on the severity of God's punishment of Miriam and Aaron. There were many people in the Bible that have committed horrendous sins but did not experience God's anger like Miriam and Aaron. Apparently, Moses's Ethiopian wife was very special. Here is that story.

> And Miriam and Aaron spake against Moses because of the Ethiopian woman whom he had married: for he had married an Ethiopian woman.
>
> And they said, Hath the LORD indeed spoken only by Moses? hath he not spoken also by us? And the LORD heard it.
>
> (Now the man Moses was very meek, above all the men which were upon the face of the earth.)
>
> And the LORD spake suddenly unto Moses, and unto Aaron, and unto Miriam, Come out ye three unto the tabernacle of the congregation. And they three came out.
>
> And the LORD came down in the pillar of the cloud, and stood in the door of the tabernacle, and called Aaron and Miriam: and they both came forth.
>
> And he said, Hear now my words: If there be a prophet among you, I the

LORD will make myself known unto him in a vision, and will speak unto him in a dream.

My servant Moses is not so, who is faithful in all mine house.

With him will I speak mouth to mouth, even apparently, and not in dark speeches; and the similitude of the LORD shall he behold: wherefore then were ye not afraid to speak against my servant Moses?

And the anger of the LORD was kindled against them; and he departed.

And the cloud departed from off the tabernacle; and, behold, Miriam became leprous, white as snow: and Aaron looked upon Miriam, and, behold, she was leprous."

And Aaron said to Moses, "Oh, my lord, do not punish us[b] because we have done foolishly and have sinned. Let her not be as one dead, whose flesh is half eaten away when he comes out of his mother's womb." And Moses cried to the LORD, "O God, please heal her—please." But the LORD said to Moses, "If her father had but spit in her face, should she not be shamed seven days? Let her be shut outside the camp seven days, and after that she may be brought in again." So Miriam was shut outside the camp seven days, and the people did not set out on the march till Miriam was brought in again. (Num. 12:1–15)

In the verses above, God revealed his displeasure and anger toward Aaron and Mariam. Other verses in the Bible expresses God's concern with how to treat people of color, but this objection was not in the same context.

It says in 1 Samuel 16:7, "But the Lord said to Samuel, 'Do not look on his appearance or on the height of his stature, because I have rejected him. For the Lord sees not as man sees: man looks on the outward appearance, but the Lord looks on the heart.'"

"Do not judge by appearances, but judge with right judgment" (John 7:24).

"So Peter opened his mouth and said: 'Truly I understand that God shows no partiality, but in every nation anyone who fears him and does what is right is acceptable to him'" (Acts 10: 34–35).

Chapter 3

Ethiopians Used for the Kingdom of Heaven

*And this gospel of the kingdom will
be proclaimed throughout the whole
world as a testimony to all nations,
and then the end will come.*
—Matthew 24:14

There are many specific incidents on how Ethiopians were used for the kingdom of heaven and came to the aid of God's chosen people Isarel. In 1 Kings, the foundation was laid for the Ethiopians' influence and the beginning of how God guided and directed their progress. God's intentions to spread the Word of the Lord to other countries are clear in 1 Kings 8:41–43, 2 Chronicles 6:32, and 1 Kings 8:60.

In these verses, God knew the plans he had for Ethiopia and the Ethiopian people. The central theme in each of these verses: "That all the peoples of the earth may know that the Lord is God, and there is no other."

In 1 Kings 8:41–43, God is referring to Ethiopia and the initial movement of the Gospel geographically and ethnically to the rest of the world. While some of the historical details of these accounts may be difficult to keep track, this book focus on the accounts that are clear, understandable, and applicable.

We can see that God takes the long view of history; nothing ever catches him by surprise. God arranges circumstances and events in order to achieve his long-range purpose to gather his children for their permanent home on Mount Zion.

Part 1
Foreigners from a Distant Land Prophesied to Visit Israel
(1 Kings 8:41–43)

> As for the foreigner who does not belong to your people Israel but has come from a distant land because of your name for they will hear of your great name and your mighty hand and your outstretched arm—when they come and pray toward this temple, then hear from heaven, your dwelling place. Do whatever the foreigner asks of you, so that all the peoples of the earth may know your name and fear you, as do your own people Israel, and may know that this house I have built bears your Name. (1 Kings 8:41–43)

This initial goal of spreading the Word of God to other countries is set in this verse. King David and his son, King Solomon, was given the necessary wisdom by God to prepare Israel for this mission. King David knew the mission and wanted to prepare his son as revealed in 1 Chronicles.

David said, "My son Solomon is young and inexperienced, and the house to be built for the LORD should be of great magnificence and fame and splendor in the sight of all the nations. Therefore I will make preparations for it." So David made extensive preparations before his death. (1 Chron. 22:5)

Part 2
The Queen of Sheba Visits Solomon
(1 King 10:1–13)

God begins the movement of the Word of God and the Gospel to other lands in 1 Kings with Queen Sheba. Up until this time, the Word of God had been confined to Isarel. Queen Sheba became interested in the wisdom of Solomon and sending her to Isaraeal served God's purpose to spread the Gospel.

Queen Sheba's visit to King Solomon in the Old Testament will subsequently be used to condemn Jesus's generation. We go from the New Testament in Matthew to the beginning of the story in 1 Kings 10:1–13 and make the connection.

How amazing that Jesus would use an incident almost one thousand years ago to condemn his generation; he did not use an occurrence involving Israel or Egypt or any other country or people, but he used an Ethiopian to condemn his generation.

When the queen of Sheba heard about the fame of Solomon and his relationship to the LORD, she came to test Solomon with hard questions.

Arriving at Jerusalem with a very great caravan—with camels carrying spices, large quantities of gold, and precious stones—she came to Solomon and talked with him about all that she had on her mind.

Solomon answered all her questions; nothing was too hard for the king to explain to her.

When the queen of Sheba saw all the wisdom of Solomon and the palace he had built, the food on his table, the seating of his officials, the attending servants in their robes, his cupbearers, and the burnt offerings he made at the temple of the LORD, she was overwhelmed.

She said to the king, "The report I heard in my own country about your achievements and your wisdom is true.

But I did not believe these things until I came and saw with my own eyes. Indeed, not even half was told me; in wisdom and wealth you have far exceeded the report I heard. How happy your people must be! How happy your officials, who continually stand before you and hear your wisdom!

Praise be to the LORD your God, who has delighted in you and placed you on the throne of Israel. Because of the LORD's eternal love for Israel, he has made you king to maintain justice and righteousness."

And she gave the king 120 talents of gold, large quantities of spices, and precious stones. Never again were so many spices brought in as those the queen of Sheba gave to King Solomon.

(Hiram's ships brought gold from Ophir; and from there they brought great cargoes of almugwood and precious stones.

The King used the almugwood to make supports for the temple of the LORD and for the royal palace, and to make harps and lyres for the musicians. So much almugwood has never been imported or seen since that day.)

King Solomon gave the queen of Sheba all she desired and asked for, besides what he had given her out of his royal bounty. Then she left and returned with her retinue to her own country. (1 King 10:1–13)

The phrase "all that she desired" in verse 13 has been interpreted in other ancient writings as Queen Sheba desired an offspring fathered by King Solomon and left Jerusalem carrying his child. Her child was named Menelik I, and he became the ancestor of all subsequent Ethiopian monarchs.

God had a reason for using Queen Sheba to spread the Word of God to the world, and we can only speculate the other reason was the Ark of the Covenant, which will be covered in part 10 of this book. We will focus primarily on what Queen Sheba learned from her visit with King Solomon in verse 10:9.

DR. LAWRENCE E. HENRY ED.D

> Praise be to the LORD your God, who has delighted in you and placed you on the throne of Israel. Because of the LORD's eternal love for Israel, he has made you king to maintain justice and righteousness. (1 Kings 10:9)

The trip to Israel by Queen Sheba is an example of what God wanted to do for Israel under the promises of the Old Covenant. God promised Israel that if they obeyed under the Old Covenant, He would bless them so tremendously that the world would notice and give glory to the Lord God of Israel.

> Now it shall come to pass, if you diligently obey the voice of the LORD your God, to observe carefully all His commandments which I command you today, that the LORD your God will set you high above all nations of the earth... Then all peoples of the earth shall see that you are called by the name of the LORD, and they shall be afraid of you. (Deut. 28:1, 10)[1]

The significance of Queen Sheba's visit is revealed in the book of Matthew.

> *The queen of the south* shall rise up in the judgment with this generation, and shall condemn it: for she came from the

---

[1] https://www.blueletterbible.org/search/preSearch.cfm?Criteria=Deuteronomy+28.1&t=NKJV.

uttermost parts of the earth to hear the wisdom of Solomon; and, behold, a greater than Solomon is here. (Matt. 12:42)

Part 3
The Queen of Sheba Visits King Solomon
(2 Chronicles 9:1–12)

This account of the queen of Sheba visit with King Solomon in 2 Chronicle 9:1–12 is a repeat of the visit in 1 Kings 10:1–13 above. It's being repeated to recognize and highlight the importance of this contact. *It was prophesized in 1 Kings 8:41–43—God's goal and intentions for this contact.*

The Queen of Sheba Visits Solomon

When the queen of Sheba heard of Solomon's fame, she came to Jerusalem to test him with hard questions. Arriving with a very great caravan—with camels carrying spices, large quantities of gold, and precious stones—she came to Solomon and talked with him about all she had on her mind. Solomon answered all her questions; nothing was too hard for him to explain to her. When the queen of Sheba saw the wisdom of Solomon, as well as the palace he had built, the food on his table, the seating of his officials, the attending servants in their robes, the cupbearers in their robes and the burnt offerings he made at[a] the temple of the LORD, she was overwhelmed.

She said to the king, "The report I heard in my own country about your achievements and your wisdom is true. But I did not believe what they said until I came and saw with my own eyes. Indeed, not even half the greatness of your wisdom was told me; you have far exceeded the report I heard. How happy your people must be! How happy your officials, who continually stand before you and hear your wisdom! Praise be to the LORD your God, who has delighted in you and placed you on his throne as king to rule for the LORD your God. Because of the love of your God for Israel and his desire to uphold them forever, he has made you king over them, to maintain justice and righteousness."

Then she gave the king 120 talents[b] of gold, large quantities of spices, and precious stones. There had never been such spices as those the queen of Sheba gave to King Solomon.

(The servants of Hiram and the servants of Solomon brought gold from Ophir; they also brought algumwood[c] and precious stones. The king used the algumwood to make steps for the temple of the LORD and for the royal palace, and to make harps and lyres for the musicians. Nothing like them had ever been seen in Judah.)

> King Solomon gave the queen of
> Sheba all she desired and asked for; he gave
> her more than she had brought to him.
> Then she left and returned with her retinue
> to her own country. (1 Kings 10:1–13)

Jesus used the queen of Sheba as an example of a seeker. "The queen of the South will rise up in the judgment with this generation and condemn it, for she came from the ends of the earth to hear the wisdom of Solomon; and indeed a greater than Solomon is here" (Matt. 12:42).[2]

If the queen of Sheba sought Solomon and the splendor of his kingdom so diligently, *how much more* should people today seek Jesus and the glory of his kingdom? The queen of Sheba will certainly also rise up in judgment against *this* generation. *God did not specifically identify any other country or people to visit King Solomon for his wisdom other than the Ethiopian—Queen Sheba.*

Part 4
The Queen of the South (Queen Sheba) Will
Rise to Condemn this Generation

> "Unless you people see signs and
> wonders," Jesus told him. "You will never
> believe. (John 4:48)

> Again his Jewish opponents picked
> up stones to stone him, but Jesus said
> to them, "I have shown you many good

---

[2] https://www.blueletterbible.org/search/preSearch.cfm?Criteria=
Matthew+12.42&t=NKJV.

works from the Father. For which of these do you stone me? (John 10:31)

He answered, A wicked and adulterous generation asks for a sign! But none will be given it except the sign of the prophet Jonah. (Matt. 12:39)

The Queen of the south shall rise up in the judgment with this generation, and shall condemn it: for she came from the uttermost parts of the earth to hear the wisdom of Solomon; and behold, a greater than Solomon is here. (Matt. 12:42)

This generation is referring to the people that crucified Jesus and failed to acknowleged that he's the Son of God.

Queen Sheba visited King Solomon in 1 Kings 10:1–13 and 2 Chronicles 9:1–12 and is being used to condemn the generation that crucified him.

There are many miraculous signs that could have used to condemn this generation, but Jesus used the one in Luke 11:29–32. (See parts 3 and 5.)

God is making it clear that there will be a judgment of people in his generation. The judgment will include a judge who will weigh their lives according to his standards. Jesus's judgment will include witnesses that will come from across the very ages to testify toward a just judgment. The queen of the South is the queen of Sheba from 1 Kings 10; she lived *centuries* before *this generation* with whom Jesus is dealing. And yet Jesus insists that on that day of judgment, she will testify against them toward a just verdict.

This declaration by Jesus that an Ethiopian will be used to judge his generation shows again how God used Ethiopians for the kingdom of heaven.

Part 5
The Men of Ninevite Will Rise to Condemn
This Generation the Sign of Jonah

Jesus Calls his Generation a Wicked Generation

As the crowds increased, Jesus said, "This is a wicked generation. It asks for a sign, but none will be given it except the sign of Jonah."

For as Jonah was a sign to the Ninevites, so also will the Son of Man be to this generation.

The Queen of the South will rise at the judgment with the people of this generation and condemn them, for she came from the ends of the earth to listen to Solomon's wisdom; and now something greater than Solomon is here.

The men of Nineveh will stand up at the judgment with this generation and condemn it, for they repented at the preaching of Jonah; and now something greater than Jonah is here. (Luke 11:29–32)

Jonah's story is familiar to most people even those who do not profess to be Christian or Jewish. *God*[3] charged the

---

[3] https://www.cgg.org/index.cfm/fuseaction/Library.sr/CT/CGG BOOKLETS/k/421/God-Is-What.htm.

prophet Jonah to go to Nineveh—the capital of Israel's hated enemy, Assyria—to prophesy of its imminent destruction. Jonah though fleed to Joppa and boarded a ship bound for Tarshish, attempting to get as far away from God and Assyria as possible. A huge storm raged, and the ship's crew chucked Jonah into the sea after the prophet admitted that the storm was chasing him. God sent a great fish to swallow Jonah, and *after three days* and nights, it spewed him onto a beach from whence he traveled to Nineveh to proclaim God's message to the Assyrians. Amazingly, they *repented*,[4] and God promised not to destroy them. At this, the prophet pitched a fit of anger, whereupon God taught him a valuable lesson on his mercy.

The queen of the South was used to condemn Jesus's generation in the books of Matthew and Luke. No sign will be given by Jesus, and the queen of the South shall rise to condemn Jesus's generation.

These verses are all referencing the story in 1 Kings 10 and 2 Chronicles 9 concerning the queen of Sheba's visit to Solomon. The verse is also identical to Luke 11:31.[5]

In the Old and New Testament, God and Jesus performed miraculous signs, to lists a few, such as in Matthew 8:9, John 20:30, John 2:1–11, John 4:46–51, John 5:1–15, John 6:16–24, and approximately fifty-six miracles in the Old Testament. The significance of God's decision to use Queen Sheba, an Ethiopian, to judge Jesus's generation cannot be overly stated nor understood by anyone other than God the Father. This declaration by Jesus that an Ethiopian will be used to judge his generation shows again how God used Ethiopians for the kingdom of heaven.

---

[4] http://www.truegospel.org/index.cfm/fuseaction/Basics.tour/ID/7/Repentance-Belief-and-Gospel.htm.

[5] https://biblehub.com/luke/11-31.htm.

Other prophets and men of God witnessed so many miraculous signs. Men like Moses, Abraham, Noah, etc., were used by God for the benefit of the kingdom of heaven. But God used Queen Sheba, an Ethiopian.

In the Bible, we also read these epic tales of the incredible ways that God transformed people and their lives: Moses, Noah, Jonah, Jeremiah, David, Joseph, Mary, Peter, James, Matthew, Zacchaeus, Paul, Lydia, Mary Magdalene, the woman at the well, and many others. Queen Sheba was not included among these people, but apparently, her contact and knowledge gained from King Solomon was paramont and very significant to spreading knowledge of the kingdom of heaven.

Part 6
Queen Sheba Shall Rise Up in the
Judgment with This Generation

Conclusion and Significance

Matthew 12:42 and Luke 11:29–32 show the significance of the Queen of Sheba and the men of Nineveh's encounters. The visit of Queen Sheba was considered miraculous because she accepted King Solomon's God. Both the queen of the South and the men of Nineveh will stand up at the judgment with Jesus's generation and condemn them.

Jonah was a miraculous sign to the Ninevites, and they repented at the preaching of Jonah. The queen of Sheba recognized the miracle of Solomon and the wisdom she received from him and his God. Jesus was the Son of God, but the Jews did not recognized it and demanded a sign. The queen of Sheba's encounter with Solomon was considered a sign as was Jonah's three days in the belly of the fish.

"Queen Sheba shall rise up in the judgment with this generation and shall condemn it." (Matthew 12:42; Luke 11:29–32)The logical meaning is that she shall rise from the dead and stand as a witness against that generation at the day of judgment and by her example and practices, which will then be produced, condemned them, or aggravated their condemnation. This is a profound occurrence because the visit to King Solomon occurred generations prior to the New Testament.

God used the queen of Sheba for the kingdom of heaven as an example of a seeker; seekers are explained in Jeremiah 29:13, Amos 5:4, and 2 Chronicles 7:14. If the queen of Sheba sought Solomon and the splendor of his kingdoms diligently, *how much more* should people today seek Jesus and the glory of his kingdom? The queen of Sheba will certainly also rise up in judgment against *this* generation.

Part 7
Ethiopian Eunuchs and Other Eunuchs
to the Kingdom of Heaven

"³And they sang a new song before the throne and before the four living creatures and the elders. No one could learn the song except the 144,000 who had been redeemed from the earth. ⁴ These are those who did not defile themselves with women, **for the remained virgins**". (Revelations 14:3-4)

The below verses specifically address Ethiopian eunuchs and other eunuchs that were used by God for the Kingdom of Heaven. (1) The first one was Ebed-mech in Jeremiah 38:10, who actually saved Jeremiah's life by rescuing him from the pit and also Ebed-mech in Jeremiah 39:15-18 that was saved by God for rescuing Jeremiah. (2) In the book of Ester, God used the eunuch Hegai to assist Esther in becoming queen of Persia, thus saving the life of thousands of Jews. Once made queen, Esther was able to influence the king to save the Jews from the threat of Harman, the top official in the King's palace. The story of Esther is covered in the book of Esther. (3) The Ethiopian eunuch in Acts was baptized by the apostle Phillips and received the Holy Spirit. This act alone probably spread Christianity throughout Africa and beyond. The baptism of the Ethiopian eunuch is covered in Chapter 7 of this book.

God's prophecy toward eunuchs is explained in Isaiah:

Isaiah 56:3-5

"3 Neither let the son of the stranger, that hath joined himself to the Lord, speak, saying, The Lord hath utterly separated me from his people: neither let the eunuch say, Behold, I am a dry tree.

4 For thus saith the Lord unto **eunuchs** that keep my Sabbaths, and choose the things that please me, and take hold of my covenant;

5 Even unto them will I give in mine house and within my walls a place and a name better than of sons and of daughters: I will give them an everlasting name that shall not be cut off."

There were probably many other Ethiopian eunuchs used by God that were not identified in the bible, however, the few that were identified are listed above.

God clarified the classification of eunuchs in the following verse, "for there are eunuchs, who were born that way, and there are eunuchs who have been made eunuchs by others—and *there those who choose to live like eunuchs for the sake of the Kingdom of Heaven.* The one who can accept this should accept it." (Matthew 19:12) In the above verse in Revelations 14:3-4, God further explained the destination of eunuchs to the Kingdom of Heaven.

Chapter 4

Rescue of Judah by King Tirhakah of Ethiopia

(2 Kings 19:9–19)

The 2 Kings documents the Ethiopian intervention that led to the rescue of Judah and defeat of kings of Assyria.

Now Sennacherib received a report that Tirhakah, the king of Cush, was marching out to fight against him. So he again sent messengers to Hezekiah with this word: "Say to Hezekiah king of Judah: Do not let the god you depend on deceive you when he says, 'Jerusalem will not be given into the hands of the king of Assyria.' Surely you have heard what the kings of Assyria have done to all the countries, destroying them completely. And will you be delivered? Did the gods of the nations that were destroyed by my predecessors deliver them—the gods of Gozan, Harran, Rezeph and the people of Eden who were in Tel Assar? Where is the king of Hamath or the king of Arpad? Where are the kings of Lair, Sepharvaim, Hena and Ivvah"?(Isaiah 37:9; 2 Kings 19:9)

Hezekiah received the letter from the messengers and read it. Then he went up to the temple of the LORD and spread it out before the LORD. [15] And Hezekiah prayed to the LORD: "LORD, the God of Israel, enthroned between the cherubim, you alone are God over all the kingdoms of the earth. You have made heaven and earth. Give ear, LORD, and hear; open your eyes, LORD, and see; listen to the words Sennacherib has sent to ridicule the living God.

"It is true, LORD, that the Assyrian kings have laid waste these nations and their lands. They have thrown their gods into the fire and destroyed them, for they were not gods but only wood and stone, fashioned by human hands. Now, LORD our God, deliver us from his hand, so that all the kingdoms of the earth may know that you alone, LORD, are God."

King Hezekiah was, according to the Hebrew Bible, the thirteenth king of Judah between c. 715 and 686 BCE. He is considered a very righteous king by the author of the books of Kings.[6] He is also one of the most prominent kings of Judah mentioned in the Bible and is one of the kings mentioned in the genealogy of Jesus in the Gospel of Matthew.[7]

In 676 BC, the Egyptian army led by King Tirhakah of Ethiopia defended Judah against the approaching Assyrian army. In one of the first battles for Jerusalem, where God intervened and destroyed the army of Assyria, the Lord caused a rumor to be circulated amongst the Assyrians that the powerful king Tirhakah, who ruled over Ethiopia, was advancing toward Assyria. This threat to Jerusalem occured after Queen Sheba's visit to King Solomon in 1 Kings, so a relationship had already established between the two countries.

"Word reached the Assyrians that the Egyptian army led by King Tirhakah of Ethiopia was coming to attack them. When the emperor heard this, he sent a letter to King Hezekiah of Judah." That certain report Isaiah was referring was that the Egyptain army led by King Tirhakah of Ethiopia was coming to attack the Assyrians. The report delayed the attack and subsequently led to the conquest of the Assyrian army by God.

Isaiah 37:9 repeats the intervention by Tirhakah that was documented in 2 Kings 19:9.

> Now Sennacherib received a report that Tirhakah, the king of Cush, was marching out to fight against him. When he heard it, he sent messengers to Hezekiah with this word: "Say to Hezekiah king of Judah: Do not let the God you depend on deceive you when he says, 'Jerusalem will not be given into the hands of the king of Assyria.'" (Isa. 37:9)

---

6   https://en.wikipedia.org/wiki/Books_of_Kings.

7   https://en.wikipedia.org/wiki/Gospel_of_Matthew.

King Sennacherib's reaction to the message from King Tirhakah showed how harden his heart was. In response to King Sennacherib's arrogant and obvious proud response to the message, God defeated the Assyrian army.

The history surrounding King Tirhakah of Ethiopia is well-documented in the Bible and the annals of archaeology. It was an important triumph in both Hebrew and world history because Judaism, a fledgling religion during this time, was protected and allowed to evolve by a later victory of the Assyrian forces by God.

This threat by Tirhakah, King of Ethiopia (Cush) to wage war against Sennacherib, and Sennacherib's response to the threat led to the intervention and defeat of Sennacherib by God.

There are many artifacts today confirming the history behind the Assyrians threats against King Hezekiah and the intervention by the Ethiopian king. The story of King Tirhakah is just another example of how God used the Ethiopians for the kingdom of God.

A massive one-ton statue of (Taharqa) Tirhakah was found deep in Sudan. Tirhakah was a pharaoh of the twenty-fifth dynasty of Egypt and came to power c. 690 BC, controlling an empire stretching from Sudan to the Levant.

The pharaohs of this dynasty were from Nubia—a territory located in modern day Sudan and Southern Egypt.

Chapter 5

Ethiopian Ebed-Melech Saves Jeremiah

Then the king commanded Ebed-Melech
the Ethiopian, "Take thirty men from
here with you and lift Jeremiah the
prophet out of the cistern before he dies."
—Jeremiah 38:10

Jeremiah was a special prophet revealed in "the Call of Jeremiah" in the following verses. The Word of the LORD came to me, saying, "Before I formed you in the womb I knew you, before you were born I set you apart; I appointed you as a prophet to the nations" (Jer. 1:4–5).

The following verses in Jeremiah explains how Ebed-Melech, the Ethiopian, was used by God to save Jeremiah (Jer. 38:7–13; 39:15–18).

> Now when Ebed-Melech the
> *Ethiopian, one of the eunuchs* which was
> in the king's house, heard that they had
> put Jeremiah in the dungeon; the king
> then sitting in the gate of Benjamin;

Ebedmelech went forth out of the king's house, and spake to the king saying,

My Lord the King, these men have done evil in all that they have done to Jeremiah the prophet, whom they have cast into the dungeon; and he is like to die for hunger in the place where he is: for there is no more bread in the city.

Then the king commanded Ebedmelech the Ethiopian, saying, Take from hence thirty men with thee, and take up Jeremiah the prophet out of the dungeon, before he die.

So Ebed-melech took the men with him, and went into the house of the king under the treasury, and took thence old cast clouts and old rotten rags, and let them down by cords into the dungeon to Jeremiah.

And Ebed-melech the Ethiopian said unto Jeremiah, Put now these old cast clouts and rotten rags under thine armholes under the cords. And Jeremiah did so.

So they drew up Jeremiah with cords, and took him up out of the dungeon: and Jeremiah remained in the court of the prison. (Jer. 38:7–13)

Ebed-Melech, the Ethiopian, was able to save Jeremiah from the dungeon. Jeremiah was one of the major prophets of the Hebrew Bible (Old Testament of Christian Bible)[8]

---

[8]   https://en.wikipedia.org/wiki/Christian_Bible.

and critical to the kingdom of heaven and the spread of Christianity. According to Jewish tradition, Jeremiah authored the book of Jeremiah,[9] the books of Kings,[10] and the book of Lamentations[11] with the assistance and under the editorship of Baruch ben Neriah,[12] his scribe, and disciple. Judaism considers the book of Jeremiah part of its canon[13] and regards Jeremiah as the second of the major prophets.

Christianity and Islam also regard Jeremiah as a prophet, and he is respectively quoted in the New Testament, and his narrative is given in Islamic tradition. In his early ministry, Jeremiah was primarily a preaching prophet, preaching throughout Israel. He condemned idolatry, the greed of priests, and false prophets.

God had specific reasons for saving Jeremiah as he would be used for the kingdom of heaven. Many years later, God instructed Jeremiah to write down these early oracles and his other messages.

---

[9]   https://en.wikipedia.org/wiki/Book_of_Jeremiah.

[10]   https://en.wikipedia.org/wiki/Books_of_Kings.

[11]   https://en.wikipedia.org/wiki/Book_of_Lamentations.

[12]   https://en.wikipedia.org/wiki/Baruch_ben_Neriah.

[13]   https://en.wikipedia.org/wiki/Biblical_canon.

Chapter 6

God Saves the Life of Ethiopian Ebed-Melech Who Rescued Jeremiah

God instructed Jeremiah to tell Ebed-Melech. "You shall not be given into the hands of the men of whom you are afraid," says the Lord.
—Jeremiah 39:15–18

"Meanwhile the word of the LORD had come to Jeremiah while he was shut up in the court of the prison, saying, "Go and speak to Ebed-Melech the Ethiopian, saying, 'Thus saysfollowing verses mentioned in the the LORD of hosts, the God of Israel: "Behold, I will bring My words upon this city for adversity and not for good, and they shall be performed in that day before you. But I will deliver you in that day," says the LORD, "and you shall not be given into the hand of the men

of whom you are afraid. For I will surely
deliver you, and you shall not fall by the
sword; but your life shall be as a prize to
you, because you have put your trust in
Me," says the LORD."[14] (Jer. 39:15–18,
NKJV)

In this verse, God was telling Jeremiah to tell Ebed-Melech, the Ethiopian, that no harm would come to him. Ebed-Melech's life was in danger because he had saved Jeremiah from the cistern (dungeon). Ebed-Melech's life was saved because he had obeyed God and trusted in the Lord.

During this time, Jerusalem had deserted the Lord as revealed in the following verse.

Go up and down the streets of
Jerusalem, look around and consider,
search through her squares. If you can
find but one person who deals honestly
and seeks the truth, I will forgive this
city. (Jer. 5:1)

This message from the Lord to Ebed-Melech was to assure him of a recompence for his great kindness to Jeremiah because "'Thou hast put thy trust in me,' saith the Lord." God recompensed men's services according to their principles. Those who trust God in the way of duty as this good man did will find that their hope shall not fail in times of the greatest danger. This incident is another example of how God used an Ethiopian for the kingdom of God.

---

[14] https://www.bible.com/bible/114/JER.39.15.NKJV.

Chapter 7

The Apostle Phillip Baptizes the Ethiopian Official- Miracle in the Desert

But you will receive power when the Holy Spirit comes on you; and you will be my witnesses in Jerusalem, and in all Judea and Samaria, and to the ends of the earth.
—Acts 1:8

The baptism of the Ethiopian official is satisfying the prophecy in Acts 1:8 and shows how Ethiopians were used to spread the good news and enhance the kingdom of God.

And the angel of the Lord spake unto Philip, saying, Arise, and go toward the south unto the way that goeth down from Jerusalem unto Gaza, which is desert.

And he arose and went: and, behold, a man of Ethiopia, an eunuch of great authority under Candace queen of the Ethiopians, who had the charge of all her treasure, and had come to Jerusalem for to worship,

Was returning, and sitting in his chariot read Esaias the prophet.

Then the Spirit said unto Philip, Go near, and join thyself to this chariot.

And Philip ran thither to him, and heard him read the prophet Esaias, and said, Understandest thou what thou readest?

And he said, How can I, except some man should guide me? And he desired Philip that he would come up and sit with him.

The place of the scripture which he read was this, He was led as a sheep to the slaughter; and like a lamb dumb before his shearer, so opened he not his mouth. (Acts 8:26–32)

In this passage, which depicts the Messiah as the suffering servant, reinforces two of the major themes of Christianity: that the Messiah's suffering was good news and that it is the purpose of God and the fulfillment of Scripture.

In his humiliation his judgment was taken away: and who shall declare his generation? for his life is taken from the earth.

And the eunuch answered Philip, and said, I pray thee, of whom speaketh the prophet this? of himself, or of some other man?

> Then Philip opened his mouth, and began at the same scripture, and preached unto him Jesus.
>
> And as they went on their way, they came unto a certain water: and the eunuch said, See, here is water; what doth hinder me to be baptized?
>
> And Philip said, If thou believest with all thine heart, thou mayest. And he answered and said, I believe that Jesus Christ is the Son of God. (Acts 8:33–37)

Verse 37 is the most important verse because the Ethiopian confessed his faith and received the Holy Spirit.

> And he commanded the chariot to stand still: and they went down both into the water, both Philip and the eunuch; and he baptized him.
>
> And when they were come up out of the water, the Spirit of the Lord caught away Philip, that the eunuch saw him no more: and he went on his way rejoicing". (Acts 8:38–39)

Though Philip was taken away *suddenly*, the Ethiopian went on his way *rejoicing*. *Joy* is a manifestation of a person's salvation (Luke 8:8, 6:23, 10:20) particularly of reception of the Holy Spirit (Acts 13:52).

It is interesting to learn that the Ethiopian was of great authority under Candace, Queen of Ethiopia. Her contact with the apostle Phillips was related to the visit of Queen

Sheba to King Solomon in 1 Kings 10:1–13. During both of these contacts, they learned of the Lord our God.

An Ethiopian received salvation with the Word of God on a lonely road from Jerusalem. This contact will affect the spread of Christianity to Ethiopia, Africa, and the world for years to come.

The traveling Ethiopian was an individual of great means, educated, literate, and wealthy. He had chosen to take a very long and potentially dangerous trip from his homeland to Jerusalem. Not only that, but he owned a chariot and was wealthy enough to be driven in this chariot.

This contact with the apostle Phillips had great relevance in the spread of Christianity to Ethiopia and Africa. This contact is clear in Acts and gives meaning to the verse, "But you will receive power when the Holy Spirit comes on you; and you will be my witnesses in Jerusalem, and in all Judea and Samaria, and to the ends of the earth" (Acts 1:8).

God is actively fulfilling his purposes for the scope of the church's mission (Luke 24:47; Acts 1:8). If it reaches an Ethiopian so soon after its beginning, what is written in 1 Kings 8:41-43, the Gospel that is to be preached among all the nations will come true.

This scene is a fitting climax to the Grecian Jewish Christians' mission thrust, for here they complete the geographical aspects of the Acts 1:8 commission. Further, it is a harbinger of the full-fledged Gentile mission to come.

In immediate obedience with little information but complete trust in the God who guides, Philip set out. For God to summon Philip from a thriving ministry in Samaria to the wilderness of the Judean hills was not an irrational move. God's goal was not only *quantity* but also *quality* in the sense of an ethnically diverse body of Christ.

Even today when four of six billion have yet to hear the Gospel within their own language and culture, we should not be surprised to see God calling evangelists to go to remote places. And like Philip, they should obey immediately and unquestioningly.

The conversion of the Ethiopian graphically demonstrates the inclusiveness of the Gospel and can also be seen as an immediate step between Jews and Gentiles. No apparent obstacle—whether physical defect, race, or geographical remoteness—can place a person beyond the saving call of the good news. Athanasius, in his comments on Psalm 68:31, marvels that "By Kushite's God indicates the end of the earth... For how Cush ran to the preaching is possible to see from the believing Ethiopian. God shows that all the other nations also believe in Christ with their kings."

For persons of black African lineage, the Ethiopian conversion and Queen Sheba's acceptance mean the "inclusion of black Africans among the charter members of the faith...all of which symbolizes from the beginning the Ethiopian involvement in the new faith that spread throughout the world."

The central theme to Acts 8 is the baptism of the Ethiopian, which is very significant because the Bible only recognized three people by name that were baptized—Christ, Simon, and John. Other then Christ none of the others was singled out and a story connected to the baptism. The Ethiopians' reaction after the baptism: "When they came up out of the water, the Spirit of the Lord suddenly took Philip away, and the eunuch did not see him again, *but went on his way rejoicing*" (Acts 8:39). "Went on his way rejoicing is an indication that the Ethiopian had received the Holy Spirit."

This miraculous event and the baptism of the Ethiopian is another example of how God used the Ethiopian for the kingdom of heaven.

Chapter 8

Ethiopia Shall Stretch Out Her Hands unto God— They Are Children of God

Are ye not as children of the Ethiopians unto me, O children of Israel? saith the Lord. Have not I brought up Israel out of the land of Egypt? And the Philistines from Caphtor, and the Syrians from Kir.
—Amos 9:7

In Amos 9:7, God is acknowledging the Ethiopians as his children.

I will record Rahab and Babylon among those who acknowledge me— Philistia too, and Tyre, along with Cush—and will say, "This one was born in Zion." (Ps. 87:4)

> Princes shall come out of Egypt;
> Ethiopia shall soon stretch out her hands
> unto God" (Ps. 68:31–32)

Even in the Old Testament, God is claiming Ethiopians as his children, and it's clear that Ethiopia will submit to God and become the willing seeker after grace, eagerly desiring and embracing God.

In Psalms 87:4 above, God is acknowledging that Ethiopia will be recorded in the Book of Life in Mount Zion. God reveals his love for his children and reminds us that there is no distinction between people, for the same Lord is Lord of all.

> He came to that which was his own, but his own did not receive him. Yet to all who did receive him, to those who believed in his name, he gave the right to become children of God children born not of natural descent, nor of human decision or a husband's will, but born of God. (1 John 11–13)

> So in Christ Jesus you are all children of God through faith, for all of you who were baptized into Christ have clothed yourselves with Christ. There is neither Jew nor Gentile, neither slave nor free, nor is there male and female, for you are all one in Christ Jesus. If you belong to Christ, then you are Abraham's seed, and heirs according to the promise. (Gal. 3:26–29)

Herds of camels will cover your land,
young camels of Midian and Ephah. And
all from Sheba will come, bearing gold
and incense and proclaiming the praise
of the LORD. (Isa. 60:6)

Yet to all who did receive him, to
those who believed in his name, he gave
the right to become children of God.
(John 1:12)

Praise be to the Lord your God,
who has delighted in you and placed
you on the throne of Israel. Because of
the Lord's eternal love for Israel, he has
made you king to maintain justice and
righteousness. (1 Kings 10:9)

In this verse, Queen Sheba is praising God and express-
ing her feelings toward the Lord.

There are other verses such as Galatians 3:14 and
Ephesian 2:8–9 that define God's children and his love for all.

The existence and emergence of Ethiopia is contempo-
raneous with creation. This phenomenon encompasses the
whole Ethiopian era of over seven thousand years of age that
extends from the days of Adam and Eve.

God seems to have bestowed on the Ethiopian the spirit
of goodness and crowned them with the life of sovereignty
inherently characterized by free will and self-determination.
Then he sealed the bond of love he built between them and
himself with a covenant that he continuously enhanced
through parallel acts of benevolence. This can be seen in how

he used Ethiopia for the kingdom of heaven as revealed in part 3 of this book and the prophecies against Cush in part 6.

Ethiopia became the faithful servants of the divine will as exemplified in the unflinching commitment to the holy covenant that was finally eternalized by Jesus Christ.

Ethiopia was singled out (Isa. 18:1–7) in the past, at the present, and in the future from among the human communities on Earth not only as true descendent of those faithful patriarchs but also as the custodians and proponents of the holy covenant.

A strong argument can be made that Ethiopia is the people and nation that qualifies for the tenure of the privileges of the divine life of perpetuity. As a result, they acquired the prerogative to declare to the world that no being is capable of challenging, corrupting, abusing, altering, or amending let alone destroying the integrity and eternity of the holy covenant that was made between God and those personages entitled to be called "his children" right from its foundation and throughout the eschatological process of its formation to its ultimate completion. Refer to Amos 9:7.

All attempts in the past at conquering, controlling, or eliminating Christianity in Ethiopia have failed thus making it the most populace Christian nation in the world.

This book has embarked on a mission of revealing and disseminating this divine truth about Ethiopia's entity as the people of God and possibly the holy covenant. As revealed in chapter 14 of this book, based on Jewish biblical tradition and Ethiopian legend via Kebra Nagast, it's believed that Israel's King Solomon together with Ethiopian Queen of Sheba conceived a child which began the Solomonic line of kings in Ethiopia, rendering the Ethiopian people as the true children of Israel and thereby chosen. Cush (Ethiopia) is *repeated* in the authorized version of the Bible too many times to count.

Chapter 9

The Spread of Christianity to Ethiopia and Beyond

Then the LORD said, "Shall I hide
from Abraham what I am about to do?
Abraham will surely become a great
and powerful nation, and all nations
on earth will be blessed through him."
—Genesis 18:17–18

The birth of Jesus was actually prophezied in the Old Testament when God made a covenant with Abraham. *Christianity is Judaism-fulfilled*—the fulfillment of promises made to Israel and the climax of God's plan of salvation.

Ethiopia was key in the spread of the Gospel when God set the foundation for using Ethiopia and the Ethiopian people to preserve and spread Christianity.

God outlined his initial plan to spread his Word to the world in the following verses:

As for the foreigner who does not
belong to your people Israel but has come
from a distant land because of your name

for they will hear of your great name and your mighty hand and your outstretched arm, when they cme and pray toward this temple, then hear from heaven, your dwelling place. Do whatever the foreigner asks of you, so that all the peoples of the earth may know your name and fear you, as do your own people Israel, and may know that this house I have built bears your Name. (1 Kings 8:41–43)

The next phase in this process of spreading the good news to the world was when the queen of Sheba heard about the fame of Solomon and his relationship to the LORD, she came to test Solomon with hard questions. Queen Sheba's visit to King Solomon actually started the spread of the good news to the world and was God-inspired.

Ethiopia (the upper Nile region) saw vibrant church growth in the early centuries, linking this growth to Philip's convert. The history of Christianity in Africa probably began during the earthly ministry of Jesus Christ two thousand years ago.

The New Testament of the Bible mentions several events in which Africans were witnesses to the life of Christ and the ministry of the apostles. It is possible that the history of Christianity in Africa began when these Africans shared what they witnessed with other Africans.

The Gospel of Luke records that a Cyrenian (northern Africa) was compelled to bear the cross for Jesus prior to Jesus's crucifixion. The book of Acts records that on the day of Pentecost, Egyptians and Cyrenians were among the crowd and heard the apostles proclaim the Gospel in their native languages. Acts also records the conversion of an influential Ethiopian eunuch to Christianity. Finally, the book of Acts records that following the apostles missionary journey to Cyprus, new converts from Cyprus and Cyrene preached the Gospel to the Greeks of Antioch. All these encounters with Africans aided in the spread of Christianity to Africa.

The spread of Christianity throughout Egypt and northern Africa during the first five centuries was rapid and intense despite the prevalence of false teachings, persecutions, and martyrdom. Some religious scholars believe that Christianity was introduced to Africans by way of the Egyptian city of Alexandria. Reportedly, the city boasted a very large Jewish community, which was located in close proximity to Jerusalem.

It is believed that African Jews in Alexandria were converted from Judaism to Christianity following a Jewish revolt in AD 115 that all but extinguished Judaism from the region.

Africans were the first to receive and embrace the Gospel of Jesus Christ. The early church in North Africa went through severe persecutions AD 64 through AD 311. In response, the church established the Catechetical (basic Christian religious education) School of Alexandria among other similar schools of Christian instruction. Many significant leaders of the faith emerged from the early African church.

Persecutions in Egypt resulted in the dispersion of Christians to the innermost regions of Egypt. Egyptian churches spread the Gospel in the Coptic (Egyptian) language and planted churches throughout the interior of Egypt. However, Christianity in the region was weakened by theological and doctrinal controversies.

The start of the seventh century, the Coptic church had established itself as the national church and had penetrated every region of the country. Although Christianity began in North Africa several centuries before its introduction in Egypt, the church in North Africa did not grow as quickly because the North African church used the Latin language in its services and literature rather than the language of the people.

An influx of muslims into the continent of Africa during the Middle Ages resulted in an exponential increase in Islamic converts, which forced many African Christians to flee to Europe. Missionary efforts by the Roman Catholic church and the European Protestant church reclaimed some of the African continent for Christ; however, Islam remains the predominant religion on the continent with Christians comprising just over 30 percent of the African population.

Egypt claims even earlier Christian visitors: Jesus and his parents who fled to Egypt to escape the murderous King Herod (Matt. 2:13–18). These visits were also recorded in Hosea 11:1. Though no churches or converts were linked to this episode, it is remembered in the Coptic liturgy, which states, "Be glad and rejoice, O Egypt, and her sons and all her borders, for there hath come to Thee the Lord of Man (Jesus)." We know that Jesus spend some time in Egypt satisfying the prophecy in Matthew.

> When they had gone, an angel of the Lord appeared to Joseph in a dream. "Get up," he said, "take the child and his mother and escape to Egypt. Stay there until I tell you, for Herod is going to search for the child to kill him."
>
> So he got up, took the child and his mother during the night and left for Egypt, where he stayed until the death of Herod. And so was fulfilled what the

Lord had said through the prophet: Out
of Egypt I called my son. (Matt. 2:13–15)

There were many avenues by which Christianity spread
into Africa. In North Africa, Christanity spread slowly west
from Alexandria and east to Ethiopia. Through North Africa,
Christianity was embraced as the religion of dissent against
once the expanding Roman Empire. In the fourth century
AD, the Ethiopian King Ezana made Christianity the kingdom's official religion.

Ancient African Christianity was basically confined to
Northern Africa—Egypt, Nubia, and Ethiopia. Churches in
these areas maintained close ties to eastern Christendom and
made many important contributions.

The seeds of the sub-Saharan church had been planted by
Western missionaries. Now as the Gospel spread throughout
the nooks and crannies of the continent, African Christianity
began to define itself on its own cultural terms. Reformers
within the missionary churches as well as independent church
leaders called for change in the institutionalized church. This
led to both reform, on the one hand, and to the birth of thousands of "African Initiated Churches" (AICs) on the other.

Christianity first arrived in North Africa in the first
or early second century AD. The Christian communities in
North Africa were among the earliest in the world. Legend
has it that Christianity was brought from Jerusalem to
Alexandria on the Egyptian coast by Mark, one of the four
evangelists, in AD 60. This was around the same time or possibly before Christianity spread to northern Europe.

Christianity spread as a popular religion across Northern
Africa, reaching into what is now Ethiopia and other regions
along the Red Sea. For a long time, it was practiced by the
people but still persecuted widely by various kingdoms and

states, including those areas controlled by the Romans. So it was largely practiced in secret. This began to change in the fourth century. In what is now Ethiopia was an extremely powerful kingdom called Axum, which drew its wealth and power from international trade routes along the Red Sea.

Axum was ruled by a man named King Ezana, who around 327 CE became one of the first rulers in the world to make Christianity the official religion of his kingdom.

Axum was the first African kingdom to fully embrace Christianity, and it became a major center for the religion as well as home to the Ethiopian Orthodox Church. As a wealthy, powerful, and internationally-respected state in many ways, it was seen as the first real Christian success story and ideal model for other kingdoms.

King Ezana of the Ethiopian/Eritrean Kingdom of Axum gave Christianity official status and facilitated the establishment of the Ethiopian Orthodox Tewahedo Church.

King Ezana's Stela above is an obelisk in the ancient city of Axum, Ethiopia.[15] The monument stands at the center of the Northern Stelae Park, which contains hundreds of smaller and less decorated stelae. This stela is probably the last one erected and the largest of those that remain unbroken.

King Ezana of Axum's Stela[16] stands 21 m (69 ft) tall, smaller than the collapsed 33 m (108 ft) Great Stela and the better-known 24 m (79 ft) Obelisk of Axum (reassembled and unveiled on September 4, 2008). It is decorated with a false door at its base and apertures resembling windows on all sides.

King Ezana ruled in the fourth century. He was the first Axumite ruler to embrace Christianity, but the inscription on the stone is from the pagan era as Ezana called himself the son of the deity Mahrem, and the Christian God is not mentioned. He fought against the Nubians and commemorated his victories on stone tablets written in Ge'ez (the ancient Eritrean/Ethiopian language), Sabaean (South Arabian), and Greek in praise of God.

Historians have uncovered a public acknowledgment of the Christian faith from Ezana. The king's engravings in stone provided a trilingual monument in different languages similar to the Rosetta stone.

The Ezana Stone is a stela from the ancient Kingdom of Axum.[17] The stone monument documents various neighboring areas, including Meroë. State coins bearing King Ezana's image depict the cross after his conversion.

The Ezana Stone shone below is a monument from the ancient Kingdom of Axum, an artifact that is available to be seen today in Axum. His carvings in stone provided a trilin-

---

15 https://en.wikipedia.org/wiki/Axum.

16 https://en.wikipedia.org/wiki/Ezana_of_Axum.

17 https://en.wikipedia.org/wiki/Kingdom_of_Aksum.

gual monument in different languages similar to the Rosetta Stone. The stone monument definitively documents the conversation of King Ezana to Christianity and his subjugation of various neighboring areas, including Meroë. *It is one of the few ancient written records to come from pre-Islamic Africa, Egypt being the other major source of inscriptions.*

The Kingdom of Axum in present-day Ethiopia and Eritrea was one of the first Christian countries in the world, having officially adopted Christianity[18] as the state religion in the fourth century. Ethiopia was the only region of Africa to survive the expansion of Islam as a Christian state.

As mentioned earlier, Christianity became the established church of the Ethiopian Aksumite Kingdom[19] under king Ezana in the 4th century when priesthood and the sacraments were brought for the first time through a Syrian Greek named Frumentius, known by the local population in Ethiopia as "Abba Selama, Kesaté Birhan" ("Father of Peace, Revealer of Light"). As a youth, Frumentius had been shipwrecked with his brother Aedesius on the Eritrean coast. The brothers managed to be brought to the royal court, where they rose to positions of influence and baptized Emperor Ezana and converted him to Christianity.

From AD 330 to 356, King Ezana ruled the ancient Kingdom of Axum centered in the Horn of Africa. He fought against the Nubians, and commemorated his victories on stone tablets in praise of God. These liturgical epigraphs were written in various ancient languages, including the Ethiopian Semitic Geʻez, the South Arabian Sabaean, and Greek.

King Ezana sent Frumentius to Alexandria to ask the Patriarch, St. Athanasius, to appoint a bishop for Ethiopia. Athanasius appointed Frumentius, who returned to Ethiopia

---

[18] https://en.wikipedia.org/wiki/Christianity.
[19] Ibid.

as Bishop with the name of "Abune Selama". From then on, until 1959, the Pope of Alexandria, was Patriarch of All Africa, and named an Egyptian (a Copt) to be *Abuna* or Archbishop of the Ethiopian Church.

An extraordinary fact about Ethiopia is that it is the only African country that has never been colonized in its three thousand years history except the five-year lose occupation by Italy.

Italy never did completely gain control of Ethiopia during that time. The Italians attempted to colonize Ethiopia twice but failed at both attempts. First, it was in 1896. Their efforts came down to a phenomenal battle at Adwa. They were utterly defeated, and Italy became the first country to recognize Ethiopia's independence and open its embassy in Addis Ababa. Second, it was in 1936 as part of WWII efforts and culminating from the forty years of shame over their defeat at the Battle of Adwa.

In the attempt to occupy Ethiopia, they occupied the capital for five years; the period referred to as "Italian occupation." Nonetheless, Ethiopian patriots fought the Italians the whole five years, and the Italians could not secure full control over the country. They were trying desperately to be recognized by the League of Nations, and the diplomatic battle too has gone on for some while.

This being so, those five years of occupation are not recognized as colonization but as an occupation during a war time.

During WWII, Netherlands, Belgium, Luxembourg, France, Denmark, Yugoslavia, Greece, Norway, and Western Poland had been occupied by the Nazis for varied periods, but they are not *colonized* per se. Same logic works with Italy and Ethiopia.

In 1941, the Italians were driven out, and Ethiopia's independence was restored from the occupation, not from the nonexistent colonization. Ethiopia observes this restoration of independence and the fight of the patriots on the Day of Patriots, which falls on May 5.

Part 8
The Ezana Stone

This stone tablet situated in a field and well below today's ground surface is believed to have been erected some time during the first half of the fourth century of the current era by King Ezana of Axum in what is now called Ethiopia. The stone monument documents the conversion of King Ezana to Christianity and his conquest of various neighboring areas, including Meroë.

The monument is interesting for several reasons. First, it is one of the few ancient written records to come from pre-Islamic Africa; Egypt being the other source of inscriptions. Second, the text on the Ezana Stone is written in several languages. This monument is trilingual: Greek, which at the time was the lingua franca in many parts of the ancient world; Ge'ez, an ancient Ethiopian language that is still a liturgical language of the Ethiopian Orthodox Church and others; and Sabaean, an Old South Arabian language used in what is now Yemen and in parts of Eritrea and northern Ethiopia.

The stone stands more or less where it was originally erected (or at least where it came to rest in antiquity) instead of gracing a hushed and elegant museum gallery in, say, Rome, Berlin or London, or, God forbid, a billionaire's private collection.

Some more interesting information about the Kingdom of Axum is that it was a trading nation in the area of Eritrea and Northern Ethiopia. It existed from approximately AD 100 to 940 and grew from the Proto-Aksumite Iron Age period in the fourth century BC to achieve prominence by the AD first century.

The Kingdom of Axum was a major player in the commercial route between the Roman Empire and Ancient India.

In addition to teaching Ezana, the monk had played decisive role in the introduction of Christianity in Axum through offering training for people to be priests and bishops. The converts were very instrumental in spreading the Word of God for the Axumite society and other conquered territories. He was also accountable for baptizing King Ezana and his brother Sayzana.

Growing up learning religious and moral lessons, King Ezana had been attracted to Christian faith and obliged to be baptized. After being baptized, the king had changed his name to Abraha meaning in Ge'ez language "light bearer." Thus, after he took his father's throne, he declared Christianity as state religion of his kingdom.

Since then, King Ezana became the first king in Africa to receive Christianity and made his kingdom the first Christian kingdom in the continent. He minted coins with the sign of cross on them so as to spread his religion throughout his kingdom and neighboring kingdoms and trading partners. Due to this, the coinsawere noted as the first coins ever found in the world to possess the Christian symbol.

King Ezana will be remembered for his effort to adopt Christianity and changing the minds of the people who believe in polytheistic religion into Christian. Through his wisdom and skillful leadership, he had managed to achieve the transformation.

Beyond declaring Christianity, King Ezana had influenced to succeeding generations many remarkable accomplishments. He made his kingdom one of the four superpowers of that time, achieving strenght economically, politically, and militarily during his rule.

> Aksum was very dominant in all sectors. It controlled the Red Sea route which continues as the busiest trading channels till this time. Coins which were minted by King Ezana, and which were later found in India and Greek showcase how much strong the Kingdom was. Not only this, he is credited for the expansion of Aksum's territory up to present day Sudan, Somalia, Kenya, and Southern Arabia. (Wikipedia, Kingdom of Aksum)

King Ezana was wise enough to record his personal achievements and the success of his kingdom in curved stones (the Ezana Stone). He used to write on carved stone in Ge'ez (which was the official language of the kingdom), Greek, and Sabean languages. He used to record his battle front adventures and other administrative issues.

The stela was magnificently carved pillar, which contained ancient mystery. It depicts his conversion to Christianity and his declaration Christian faith as his state religion and his remarkable victory over the Cush, a powerful neighboring kingdom of that time. Any tourist who wants to bear eye witness to Axum could pay homage to the stela standing upright today.

As expressed above, Ezana was successful in military feats. He had conquered many kingdoms in East Africa using his mightiest military power.

The whole of Red Sea route was under his control. According to Yonas, the Kingdom of Meroë (Nubia), which is now Sudan, was a competitor of Aksumite kingdom. Having understood this, King Ezana declared war on Meroë and achieved colorful a victory. The victory gained there had helped him to expand his territory and to control more resources and trade routes.

The historian, Yonas Kebede, hails King Ezana's diplomatic skills. He was very smart in persuading the defeated leaders and society to come together for common interest. Likewise, his wise treatment of those people who were colonized after fierce battles was highly admired. They were safe from slavery, discrimination, and oppression as long as they proved willing to respect the rules and regulations of the kingdom. As he was very humble and generous king, he used to resettle them in fertile land around Axum and allow them to assimilate with Aksumite societies.

"It was really unthinkable at that time a king would treat his subjects in such a civilized manner. His leadership wisdom had entitled him to conquer more territories and to expand trade transactions," he insisted. Besides, King Ezana is known by his granite obelisks, which are still standing in the city of Axum.

Ezana is also praised for finding the *Ark of the Covenant* from Tana Qirqos near Bahir Dar, Amhara State's capital. He brought it back to Axum to be secretly housed or placed in the *Cathedral of St. Mary of Zion*, which was built by him.

See the image of the cathedral below.

Cathedral of St. Mary of Zion[20]

---

[20] https://www.flickr.com/photos/45206671@N00/22712076051.

Chapter 10

Prophecies against Cush (Ethiopia)

Trumpet sounds, banner is raised,
branches cut, harvest begin, and
God's dwelling place defined.
—Isaiah 11:10; 1 Cor 15:51-53;
Rev 1:10, 11:15, 4:1; Joel 2:1;
Rev 21:3; Zech 2:10; Ps 132:13;
Isaiah 18:5; Matt 13:30; John 15:1

Each of the following verses mentioned in the prophecy to Ethiopia pertain to *signs* that Ethiopians must be aware of prior to the coming of the Lord at Mount Zion.

---

1. Isaiah 11:10–11
2. 1 Corithians 15:51–53
3. Matthew 24:31–41
4. Revelation 1:10
5. Revelation 11:15
6. Revelation 4:1
7. Psalm 47:5
8. Joel 2:1–2
9. Revelation 21:3
10. 2 Corinthians 1–2
11. Ephesians 2:21–22
12. Deuteronomy 26:15

13. Zechariah 2:10–13
14. Matthew 9:38
15. John 15:1–17
16. Revelation 14:15

17. Matthew 13:30–40
18. Jeremiah 7:33
19. Ezekiel 39:17–20
20. Isa. 18:1–7

I am telling you now before it happens, so that when it does happen you will believe that I am who I am. (John 13:19)

So be on your guard; I have told you everything ahead of time. (Mark 13:23)

Cush (Hebrew) was, according to the Bible,[21] the eldest son of Ham,[22] a son of Noah.[23] He was the brother of Canaan[24] (land of Canaan), Mizraim[25] (Egypt) and Phut[26] (land of Libya), and the father of the biblical Nimrod mentioned in the "Table of Nations"[27] in Genesis 10:6[28] and 1 Chronicles 1:8.[29]

Cush is traditionally considered the eponymous ancestor of the people of the "land of Cush," an ancient territory that is believed to have been located on either side or both

---

21 https://en.wikipedia.org/wiki/Bible.
22 https://en.wikipedia.org/wiki/Ham_(son_of_Noah).
23 https://en.wikipedia.org/wiki/Noah.
24 https://en.wikipedia.org/wiki/Canaan_(son_of_Ham).
25 https://en.wikipedia.org/wiki/Mizraim.
26 https://en.wikipedia.org/wiki/Phut.
27 https://en.wikipedia.org/wiki/Table_of_Nations.
28 https://en.wikipedia.org/wiki/Book_of_Genesis.
29 https://en.wikipedia.org/wiki/I_Chronicles.

sides of the Red Sea.[30] As such, Cush is alternately identified in scripture with the Kingdom of Cush[31] or ancient Ethiopia.

The Cushitic languages[32] are named after Cush.

The Bible mentions Ethiopia and Ethiopians many times and on each occasion they were used to protect and expand the *kingdom of heaven.*

The most important scriptures that deals with Ethiopian prophecy is in Isaiah 18:1–7. These prophecies are important because it fulfills what is written in Luke 24:44: "He said to them, this is what I told you while I was still with you: Everything must be fulfilled that is written about me in the Law of Moses, the Prophecy and the Psalms."

The prophecy against Cush is the only place that specifically addresses people and nation other than Israel and Egypt.

There is very little mention of other nations or people. In these scriptures, God is telling the Ethiopians what is expected of them at the end times. The oracles against other nations in Isaiah do not come close to matching the oracles against Ethiopia.

The oracles against Ethiopia gave explicit instructions when Jesus came to Mount Zion and established his children a permanent home. Ethiopians had been given tasks to perform for the kingdom of heaven. God even gave them the signs to watch for so they could be prepared.

From all indications, as revealed in Isaiah 18:1–7, Isaiah 56:1–2, Amos 9:7, and Acts 8:38, God will not forget the Ethiopians who labored to protect the kingdom of heaven— Ethiopians such as Queen Sheba, the Ethiopian baptized by the apostle Phillip, the Ethiopian that saved Jeremiah, the

---

[30] https://en.wikipedia.org/wiki/Red_Sea.
[31] https://en.wikipedia.org/wiki/Kingdom_of_Kush.
[32] https://en.wikipedia.org/wiki/Cushitic_languages.

Ethiopian King Tirhakah that saved Judah, and others that are unnamed.

Prophecies against Ethiopia are very specific and detailed, including the meaning of signs such as banner, trumpet, vines, branches, and an explanation of his dwelling place. These details are not included in any of the prophecies to other nations or people.

> Woe to the land of whirring wings along the rivers of Cush, ² which sends envoys by sea in papyrus boats over the water. Go, swift messengers, to a people tall and smooth-skinned, to a people feared far and wide, an aggressive nation of strange speech whose land is divided by rivers. (Isa. 18:1–2)

Verses 1 and 2 are referring to the location and description of the Cushites (Ethiopians).

In Isaiah 18:1 (NIV), people who are tall and have smooth skin were probably the people of Cush and Egypt. The reference to smooth-skinned people were also mentioned in the book of Genesis when Rebekah was trying to get Isaac's blessings for Jacob. "Jacob said to Rebekah his mother, 'But my brother Esau is a hairy man while I have smooth skin'" (Gen. 27:11).

> All you people of the world, you who live on the earth, when a banner is raised on the mountains, you will see it, and when a trumpet sounds, you will hear it, when a *banner* is raised on the mountains, you will see it. (Isa. 18:3)

This verse reminds the Cushites of the meaning and importance of the *banner* and *trumpet* sounding.

The banner and trumpet are referred to in numerous other verses are all referring to Jesus' return:

> In that day the Root of Jesse will stand as a *banner* for the peoples; the nations will rally to him, and his resting place will be glorious. In that day the Lord will reach out his hand a second time to reclaim the surviving remnant of his people from Assyria, from Lower Egypt, from Upper Egypt, from Cush, from Elam, from Babylonia, from Hamath and from the islands of the Mediterranean. (Isa. 11:10–11; italics mine)

> Listen, I tell you a mystery: We will not all sleep, but we will all be changed—in a flash, in the twinkling of an eye, at the last *trumpet*. For the *trumpet* will sound, the dead will be raised imperishable, and we will be changed. For the perishable must clothe itself with the imperishable, and the mortal with immortality. (1 Cor. 15:51–53; italics mine)

> And he will send his angels with a loud *trumpet* call, and they will gather his elect from the four winds, from one end of the heavens to the other. "Now learn this lesson from the fig tree: As soon as its twigs get tender and its leaves come out,

you know that summer is near. Even so, when you see all these things, you know that it is near, right at the door. Truly I tell you, this generation will certainly not pass away until all these things have happened. Heaven and earth will pass away, but my words will never pass away." (Matt. 24:31–41; italics mine)

On the Lord's Day I was in the Spirit, and I heard behind me a loud voice like a *trumpet*. (Rev. 1:10; italics mine)

The seventh angel sounded his *trumpet*, and there were loud voices in heaven, which said: The kingdom of the world has become the kingdom of our Lord and of his Messiah, and he will reign for ever and ever. (Rev. 11:15; italics mine)

After this I looked, and there before me was door standing open in heaven. And the voice I had first heard speaking to me like a *trumpet* said, "Come up here, and I will show you what must take place after this." (Rev. 4:1; italics mine)

God has ascended amid shouts of joy, the LORD amid the sounding of *trumpets*. (Ps. 47:5; italics mine)

Blow the *trumpet* in Zion; sound the alarm on my holy hill. Let all who live tremble, for the day of the LORD is coming. It is close at hand a day of darkness gloom, a day of clouds and blackness. Like dawn spreading across the mountains a large and mighty army comes, such as never was in ancient times nor ever will be in ages to come. (Joel 2:1–2; italics mine)

God has ascended amid shouts of joy, the LORD amid the sounding of *trumpets.* (Ps. 47:5; italics mine)

For so the LORD said unto me, I will take my rest, and I will consider in my *dwelling place* like a clear heat upon herbs, and like a cloud of dew in the heat of harvest. (Isa. 18:4, KJV; italics mine)

This verse mentions Gods *dwelling* in the new Jerusalem. There are numerous other verses that collaborate this verse:

And I heard a great voice out of heaven saying, Behold, the tabernacle of God is with men, and he will *dwell* with them, and they shall be his people, and God himself shall be with them, and be their God. (Rev. 21:3; italics mine)

For we know that if the earthly tent we live in is destroyed, we have a building from God, an eternal house in heaven, not built by human hands. Meanwhile we groan, longing to be clothed instead with our *heavenly dwelling.* (2 Cor. 5:1–2, NIV)

In whom the whole building, being fitted together, grows into a holy temple in the Lord, in whom you also are being built together for a *dwelling place* of God in the Spirit. (Eph. 2:21–22, KJV; italics mine)

Look down from heaven, your holy *dwelling place,* and bless your people Israel and the land you have given us as you promised on oath to our ancestors, a land flowing with milk and honey." (Deut. 26:15, NIV; italics mine)

"Shout and be glad, Daughter Zion. For I am coming, and I will live among you," declares the LORD. "Many nations will be joined with the LORD in that day and will become my people. I will live among you and you will know that the LORD Almighty has sent me to you. The LORD will inherit Judah as his portion in the holy land and will again choose Jerusalem. Be still before the LORD, all mankind, because he has roused himself from his holy *dwelling.*" (Zech. 2:10–13; italics mine)

And I heard a loud voice from the throne saying, "Look! God's dwelling place is now among the people, and he will *dwell* with them. They will be his people, and God himself will be with them and be their God." (Rev. 21:3; italics mine)

For the LORD hath chosen Zion; he hath desired it for his *habitation*. This is my rest for ever: here will I *dwell*; for I have desired it. (Ps. 132:13–14; italics mine)

For the LORD has chosen Zion; He has desired it for His habitation. This is My resting place forever; Here I will *dwell*, for I have desired it. (Ps. 132:13–14; italics mine)[33]

For, before the *harvest*, when the blossom is gone and the flower becomes a ripening grape, he will cut off the shoots with pruning knives, and cut down and take away the spreading branches. (Isa. 18:5; italics mine)

Harvest is when we reap the benefits of living righteously. You see, the symbolic meaning of harvest in Holy Scripture encompasses two main areas: God's provision for us and God's blessing for others.

There are other verses that refer to the *harvest*:

Ask the Lord of the *harvest*, therefore, to send out workers into his harvest field. (Matt. 9:38)

---

[33] https://bible.knowing-jesus.com/Psalm/132/13.

I am the true vine, and my Father is the gardener. [2] He cuts off every *branch* in me that bears no fruit, while every *branch* that does bear fruit he prunes so that it will be even more fruitful. You are already clean because of the word I have spoken to you. Remain in me, as I also remain in you. No *branch* can bear fruit by itself; it must remain in the vine. Neither can you bear fruit unless you remain in me.

I am the vine; you are the *branches*. If you remain in me and I in you, you will bear much fruit; apart from me you can do nothing. If you do not remain in me, you are like a *branch* that is thrown away and withers; such *branches* are picked up, thrown into the fire and burned. If you remain in me and my words remain in you, ask whatever you wish, and it will be done for you. This is to my Father's glory, that you bear much fruit, showing yourselves to be my disciples.

The Hebrews and other Semitic peoples used the term *branch* in a genealogical sense, meaning that a certain person belongs to or descends from a particular family line. To give the same sense, we might use the term "heir," "descendant," "seed," or "scion." Like Hebrew, English links trees and genealogy in such phrases as "family tree" and "the apple doesn't fall very far from the tree. Branch here is referring to the root of Jesse [Jesus]. (John 15:1–17; italics mine)

Then another angel came out of the temple and called in a loud voice to him who was sitting on the cloud, "Take your sickle and reap, because the time to reap has come, for the *harvest* of the earth is ripe." (Rev. 14:15; italics mine)

Let both grow together until the *harvest*: and in the time of *harvest* I will say to the reapers, Gather ye together first the tares, and bind them in bundles to burn them: but gather the wheat into my barn.
Which indeed is the least of all seeds: but when it is grown, it is the greatest among herbs, and becometh a tree, so that the birds of the air come and lodge in the *branches* thereof.
The enemy that sowed them is the devil; the *harvest* is the end of the world; and the reapers are the angels. (Matt. 13:30, 32, 39–40, KJV; italics mine)

The Bible uses the term *harvest* when referring to rescuing of the remains of Israel and the resurrection of believers from the earth.

They will all be left to the mountain birds of prey and to the wild animals; the birds will feed on them all summer, the wild animals all winter. (Isa. 18:6)

This prophecy is also mentioned in other verses.

> Then the carcasses of this people will become food for the birds and the wild animals, and there will be no one to frighten them away. (Jer. 7:33)

> And, thou son of man, thus saith the Lord GOD; Speak unto every feathered fowl, and to every beast of the field, Assemble yourselves, and come; gather yourselves on every side to my sacrifice that I do sacrifice for you, even a great sacrifice upon the mountains of Israel, that ye may eat flesh, and drink blood.
> Ye shall eat the flesh of the mighty, and drink the blood of the princes of the earth, of rams, of lambs, and of goats, of bullocks, all of them fatlings of Bashan.
> And ye shall eat fat till ye be full, and drink blood till ye be drunken, of my sacrifice which I have sacrificed for you.
> Thus ye shall be filled at my table with horses and chariots, with mighty men, and with all men of war, saith the Lord GOD. (Ezek. 39:17–20, KJV)

The nature of the gift is unknown. Some literature speculate that the Ark of the Covenant is maintained in Ethiopia under the care of Ethiopian eunuchs in the church of mount Zion in Axum and will be given to God in end of times. The Ark of the Covenant is mentioned in Revelation 11:19.

Chapter 11

Gifts to God from Ethiopia to Mount Zion from People of Smooth Skin Bibilical Description of Jesus

Prophecy to Cush:

> Which sends envoys by sea in papyrus boats over the water. Go, swift messengers, to a people tall and smooth-skinned, to a people feared far and wide, an aggressive nation of strange speech, whose land is divided by rivers. (Isa. 18:2)

> At that time the LORD of Heaven's Armies will receive gifts from this land divided by rivers, from this tall, smooth-skinned people, who are feared far and wide for their conquests and destruction. They will bring the gifts to Jerusalem, where the LORD of Heaven's Armies dwells. (Isa. 18:7)

As mentioned earlier, gifts are offered to God at the New Jerusalem, specifically addressing the Ethiopians. These verses all refer to gifts being brought to God at the New Jerusalem and how Ethiopia became attached to God. God was prophesizing that at the end of times, Ethiopia would bring gifts to Mount Zion—the final home of our Lord.

The below verses are also reference gifts being brought to God.

> From beyond the rivers of Cush
> my worshipers, my scattered people, will
> bring me offerings. (Zeph. 3:10)

> The kings of Tarshish and of the isles
> shall bring presents: the kings of Sheba
> and Seba shall offer gifts. (Ps. 72:10)

In Isaiah 60:6 (the glory of Zion), "Herds of camels will cover your land, young camels of Midian and Ephah. And all from Sheba will come, bearing gold and incense and proclaiming the praise of the LORD."

In all the above verses, God required a gift from the Ethiopians. There was no other country that required a gift/tribute to be brought to the Lord at Zion from a nation other than Ethiopia.

The nature of the gift is unknown. Some literature speculate that the Ark of the Covenant was maintained in Ethiopia under the care of Ethiopian eunuchs in the church of mount Zion in Axum and would be given to God in end of times. The Ark of the Covenant is mentioned in Revelation 11:19 and will be located at Mount Zion.

It is prophesized in Isaiah 18 verses 2 and 7 that gifts will be offered to God at the New Jerusalem from the people of smooth skin. Smooth-skinned people are also referred in Genesis 27:11. "Jacob said to Rebekah his mother, 'But my brother Esau is a hairy man while I have smooth skin.'"

A conclusion could be made that God is trying to make the point that Jacob was also an Ethiopian, but that conclusion is only speculative.

Jacob, having smooth skin, cannot be interpreted as being of Ethiopian descendant, but it does induce the conversation. Jacob was in the descendant lifeline of Abraham and so would inherent the promise from God.

Skin color of Jesus and bloodline of the family of King David had been a topic of discussion since the days of early Christianity.[34] Various theories about the race of Jesus have been proposed and debated.

By the Middle Ages, a number of documents—generally of unknown or questionable origin—had been composed and were circulating with details of the appearance of Jesus which resulted in the interpretion of Jesus as being Caucasian. Modern day interpretation of Jesus is that he is Caucasian. The New and Old Testaments have the descriptions of Jesus.

The following verses addressed Jesus's skin color:

> His body was like topaz, his face like lightning, his eyes like flaming torches, his arms and legs like the gleam of burnished bronze, and his voice like the sound of a multitude. (Dan. 10:6)

> His feet were like bronze glowing in a furnace, and his voice was like the sound of rushing waters. 16 In his right

---

[34] https://en.wikipedia.org/wiki/Early_Christianity.

hand he held seven stars, and coming out of his mouth was a sharp, double-edged sword. His face was like the sun shining in all its brilliance. (Rev. 1:15–16)

To the angel of the church in Thyatira write: These are the words of the Son of God, whose eyes are like blazing fire and whose feet are like burnished bronze. I know your deeds, your love and faith, your service and perseverance, and that you are now doing more than you did at first. (Rev. 2:18–19)

The hair on his head was white like wool, as white as snow, and his eyes were like blazing fire. His feet were like bronze glowing in a furnace, and his voice was like the sound of rushing waters. (Rev. 1:14–15)

The birth of Esau and Jacob activates the thought process. Both were born at the same time, but Jacob was smooth skin, and Esau was born red and hairy.

Jacob eventually received Esau's birthright that supposed to have gone to Esau—the firstborn. The birthright had to do with both position and inheritance. By birthright, the firstborn son inherited the leadership of the family and the judicial authority of his father.

Rebekah and Jacob was able to successfully deceive Issac and receive Esau's birthright. Isaac blessed Jacob with the blessing that was meant for Esau. Genesis 27:28–29 states Isaac's blessing.

> Therefore God give thee of the dew
> of heavens, and the fatness of the earth,
> and plenty of corn and wine: Let people
> serve thee: be lord over thy brethren, and
> let thy mother's sons bow down to thee:
> cursed be every one that curseth thee,
> and blessed be he that blesseth thee.

The birthright was very important because it was the natural privilege of the firstborn son to become the head of the family and be in charge of the family, including the family property. He would be responsible for the welfare of the younger sons, the widow, and any unmarried daughters. He would exercise considerable authority over the other members of the family.

The blessing that he received would also place him in a special covenant relationship with the Lord.

During the patriarchal period, when Jacob and Esau lived, God dealt directly with the heads of the families. The Hebrews counted the blessing given by the Father to be very important and considered it an oral contract, which was just as binding as a written contract.

In the case of Jacob, it appears that he did not actually inherit any property from his father even though he did buy the birthright from Esau for a bowl of pottage—a kind of bean stew. What Jacob did receive from Isaac was the blessing planned for Esau. The blessing, a sort of last will and testament, promised that Jacob would have lordship over other nations. The blessing Jacob received promised him divine protection so that whoever cursed Jacob would be cursed and whoever blessed Jacob would receive the blessing of God.

Issac's blessing was given to Jacob in the following verses:

> Therefore God give thee of the dew of heaven, and the fatness of the earth, and plenty of corn and wine: Let people serve thee, and nations bow down to thee: be lord over thy brethren, and let thy mother's sons bow down to thee: cursed be every one that curseth thee, and blessed be he that blesseth thee. (Gen. 27:28–29)[35]

> Jacob's name was changed to Israel and eventually he received the covenant from God. 28 Then the man said, "Your name will no longer be Jacob, but Israel, because you have struggled with God and with humans and have overcome." (Gen. 32:28)

In Judaism,[36] "chosenness" is the belief that the Jews,[37] via descent from the ancient Israelites, are the chosen people[38] (i.e., chosen to be in a covenant with God).

The idea of the Israelites being chosen by God is found most directly in the book of Deuteronomy. God promised to make Abraham the father of a great people and said that Abraham and his descendants must obey God. In return, God would guide them and protect them and give them the land of Israel. Isaac was the descendant from Abraham to receive the covenant.

---

[35] https://biblia.com/bible/kjv1900/Gen%2027.28-29.

[36] https://en.wikipedia.org/wiki/Judaism.

[37] https://en.wikipedia.org/wiki/Chosen_people.

[38] Ibid.

Chapter 12

Modern-Day Christianity in Ethiopia and Africa

But you will receive power when the
Holy Spirit comes on you; and you
will be my witnesses in Jerusalem,
and in all Judea and Samaria,
and to the ends of the earth.
—Acts 1:8

Approximately 64.1 percent of the
112.08 million people in Ethiopia are
Christians.

All of the prophecies that was
fulfilled by Ethiopia has the benefit
of spreading the gospel to the world.
(Wikipedia, Christianity in Ethiopia)

In Ethiopia, the most prominent and longstanding religion had been the Ethiopian Orthodox Tewahedo Church[39]

---

[39] https://en.wikipedia.org/wiki/Ethiopian_Orthodox_Tewahedo_Church.

(then including the Eritrean Orthodox Tewahedo Church)[40] since the times of St. Frumentius.[41]

St. Frumentius (Ge'ez: "Fremnāṭos") was born in Tyre,[42] eastern Roman Empire in the early fourth century, who died circa 383 in Kingdom of Axum; was the first bishop of Axum; and is credited with bringing Christianity to the Kingdom of Axum. He was sometimes known by other names such as Abuna (our father) and Aba Selama.

The Ethiopian Orthodox Tewahedo Church is the largest of the Oriental Orthodox[43] Christian Churches. One of the few precolonial Christian churches in sub-Saharan Africa, the Ethiopian Orthodox Tewahedo Church, has a membership of between 45 and 50 million people—the majority of whom live in Ethiopia. It is a founding member of the World Council of Churches.[44]

The Ethiopian Orthodox Tewahedo Church is in communion with the Eritrean Orthodox Tewahedo Church, the Coptic Orthodox Church of Alexandria, the Syriac Orthodox Church, the Armenian Apostolic Church, and the Malankara Orthodox Syrian Church, having gained autocephaly in 1959.

The Ethiopian Orthodox Tewahedo Church was administratively part of the Coptic Orthodox Church of Alexandria from the first half of the fourth century until 1959 when it was granted its own patriarch by Cyril VI, pope of the Coptic Orthodox Church of Alexandria. It is one of the old-

---

[40] https://en.wikipedia.org/wiki/Eritrean_Orthodox_Tewahedo_Church.

[41] https://en.wikipedia.org/wiki/Saint_Frumentius.

[42] https://en.wikipedia.org/wiki/Tyre,_Lebanon.

[43] https://en.wikipedia.org/wiki/Oriental_Orthodoxy.

[44] https://en.wikipedia.org/wiki/World_Council_of_Churches.

est Christian churches, and as a non-Chalcedonian church,[45] it is not in full communion with the Ethiopian Catholic Church.

Ethiopia is the second country historically, following only Armenia to have officially proclaimed Christianity as state religion in AD 333.

Tewahedo is a Ge'ez word meaning "being made one." This word refers to the Oriental Orthodox belief in the one perfectly unified nature of Christ (i.e., a complete union of the divine and human natures into one nature is self-evident in order to accomplish the divine salvation of humankind as opposed to the "two natures of Christ" belief commonly held by the Roman Catholic and Eastern Orthodox, Anglican, Lutheran, and most Protestant churches).

With a 2019 population of approximately 112.08 million up from 2015's estimate of 98.9 million, Ethiopia is the most populous landlocked country in the continent of Africa and the second most populous country of Africa after Nigeria. About 62.8 percent (Orthodox, 43.5 percent; Protestant, 18 percent; and Catholic, 0.7 percent) of the people of Ethiopia are Christians, and Christianity is predominant in the north. All the southern regions have Muslim majorities, who represent about 33.9 percent of the country's population. About 64.1 percent of the 112.08 million people in Ethiopia are Christians.

For centuries, historians have widely accepted the argument that Armenia was the first Christian nation. This important claim has become a source of national pride for Armenians and has remained virtually undisputed for centuries until now.

Armenians will likely be up at arms when they learn that a new book, *Abyssinian Christianity: The First Christian*

---

[45] https://en.wikipedia.org/wiki/Council_of_Chalcedon.

Nation?, is challenging their claim, presenting the possibility that Abyssinia (modern-day Ethiopia and Eritrea) was the first Christian nation. To be sure, the book doesn't conclusively assert that Ethiopia was the first nation to adopt Christianity as its state religion. However, it will surely challenge the confidence of modern church historians with groundbreaking evidence.

According to a report on April 4, 2019, in Quartz Africa by Yomi Kazeem, Africa is set to be the global center of Christianity for the next fifty years. There are already more Christians in Africa than any other continent. By 2060, six of the countries with the top ten largest Christian populations will be in Africa up from three in 2015, according to a new Pew Research Center report.[46] The projections are in line with the gradual shift that has increasingly seen Christian populations live outside the historical cultural centers of the religion.

The size of the Christian population in Nigeria alone—already the largest on the continent—is projected to double by 2060. In addition, Tanzania, Uganda, and Kenya are projected to join the list of countries with the top ten largest Christian populations, replacing Russia, Germany, and China. In total, the Christian population in Nigeria, Congo, Tanzania, Uganda, Kenya, and Ethiopia account for just under a quarter of the projected global Christian population of three billion people.

The upsurge in the African Christian population matches general population growth projections while around 2.2 billion people could be added to the global population by 2050. More than half of that growth will occur in Africa. Meanwhile, the decline of Christian population in Europe is especially nota-

---

[46] https://www.pewresearch.org/fact-tank/2019/04/01/the-countries-with-the-10-largest-christian-populations-and-the-10-largest-muslim-populations/.

ble in Britain where, last year, a survey showed "an unrelenting decline in Church of England and Church of Scotland" numbers. Only 14 percent of Britons identified as members of the Church of England—a record low. Similarly, Church of Scotland numbers dropped to 18 percent from 31 percent in 2002.

In contrast, the spread of Christianity is clearly visible in several African countries with an explosion in the number of church denominations and structures across urban centers and even in rural areas. In some cases, megachurch sites are morphing into cities[47] complete with housing estates, banks, grocery stores, and police stations.

Beyond dominant architecture, the prominence of Christianity is often visible in other ways in Ghana. For instance, small and medium scale businesses are often named based on biblical verses.

The rise of Christianity in Africa is also captured outside the continent. In a reversal from nearly five centuries ago, when Christian missionaries first brought the religion to African communities, African preachers led by "reverse missionaries"[48] are increasingly taking charge of the Gospel in England as Quartz Africa has reported. In comparison, while there were three African countries (Nigeria, Egypt, Algeria) among countries with top ten largest Muslim populations in 2015, that number will be reduced to two (Nigeria and Egypt) by 2060. Nigeria's religious fault lines are also highlighted in the report. As by 2060, it will be home to the third largest Muslim and Christian populations globally and will

---

[47] https://www.theguardian.com/cities/2017/sep/11/eat-pray-live-lagos-nigeria-megachurches-redemption-camp.

[48] https://qz.com/africa/1088489/africas-reverse-missionaries-are-trying-to-bring-christianity-back-to-the-united-kingdom/.

be the only country on the list on top ten largest populations for both religions.

Bete Giyorgis, part of the Lalibela Churches in Ethiopia, are an early example of Christian architecture in Africa and are one of Africa's most significant archaeological discoveries[49]

Ethiopian monks worshipping at St. George Church[50]

---

[49] https://en.wikipedia.org/wiki/Church_of_Saint_George,_Lalibela.
[50] https://en.wikipedia.org/wiki/Lalibela.

Part 9
Christian Holidays in Ethiopia

Religious celebrations in Ethiopia are great, and colorful events frequently take place over several days. Important Christian holidays include Meskel, Christmas, Timkat, Kiddus Yohannes, and Easter.

Timkat, which marks Christ's baptism, is the most colorful event of the year. In September, the two-day feast of Meskal marks the finding of the True Cross. Kiddus Yohannes (New Year's Day) comes on September 11, which coincides with the end of the season of heavy rains and the beginning of spring.

Muslim holidays are based on the lunar calendar and fall at different times each year. The ninth month of the Muslim calendar is devoted to Ramadan, which is marked by fasting.

One of the great Muslim feasts of the year is Eid al-Fitr, which celebrates the end of Ramadan. The Eid al-Adha is the feast marking Abraham's willingness to sacrifice Isaac as commanded by God. On these days, after praying and listening to the imam (religious leader), Muslim Ethiopians sacrifice animals and distribute part of the meat to the poor. Wearing new clothes, they visit friends and relatives as well as family graves. Horse races are also traditional on these days. Muslims celebrate the prophet Muhammad's birthday on September 20 and mark the anniversaries of numerous martyrs.

Timkat is the Orthodox Tewahedo celebration of Epiphany. It is celebrated on January 19 (or 20 in a leap year), corresponding to the 10th day of Terr in the Ethiopian calendar.

Timkat celebrates the baptism of Jesus in the Jordan River. This festival is best known for its ritual reenactment of baptism (similar to such reenactments performed by numerous Christian pilgrims to the holy land when they visit the Jordan).

Ethiopian Tewahedo priests at a
Timkat ceremony in Jan Meda

During the ceremonies of Timkat, the tabot,[51] a model of the Ark of the Covenant, which is present on every Ethiopian altar (somewhat like the Western altar stone), is reverently wrapped in rich cloth and burned in procession on the head of the priest. The tabot, which is otherwise rarely seen by the laity (nonordained member), represents the manifestation of Jesus as the Messiah when he came to the Jordan for baptism.

The Divine Liturgy[52] is celebrated near a stream or pool early in the morning (around 2:00 a.m.). Then the nearby body of water is blessed toward dawn and sprinkled on the participants; some of whom enter the water and immerse themselves, symbolically renewing their baptismal vows.

Easter or Fasika takes place in all the Christian Churches throughout the country whether it be Orthodox, Catholic, or Protestant and follows the eastern method of calculating Easter, thus tending to fall after Easter in the Western calendar. (Some years both fall on the same date.)

---

[51] https://en.wikipedia.org/wiki/Tabot.

[52] https://en.wikipedia.org/wiki/Divine_Liturgy.

Fasika is a much more important festival than Christmas since the death and resurrection of Jesus[53] is more significant in Orthodox and Ethiopian Evangelical theology than his birth. Jesus's crucifixion, which led to his death on a Friday, according to Orthodox thought, was for the purpose of fulfilling the Word of God and led to the conquest of death and Jesus's resurrection from the tomb after three days—the third day being the Sunday when Ethiopian Easter is celebrated.

Fasika is a climactic celebration with fasting, becoming more intense over the fifty-five-day period of Lent[54] for Orthodox Christians, Catholics, and optionally for some Protestant denominations. No meat or animal products of any kind, including milk and butter, are eaten.

Good Friday[55] starts off by church going and is a day of preparation for the breaking of this long fasting period.

The Orthodox Christians prostrate themselves in church, bowing down and rising up until they get tired.

The main religious service takes place with the Paschal Vigil[56] on Saturday night. It is a somber, sacred occasion with music and dancing until the early hours of the morning. At 3:00 a.m., everyone returns home to break their fast, and a chicken is slaughtered at midnight for the symbolic occasion. In the morning, after a rest, a sheep is slaughtered to start the feasting on Easter Sunday while Catholics and Protestant denominations have special Easter services/masses, bringing in people from various smaller community churches together to participate in an Easter sermon and celebration.

In Ethiopian-Eritrean Orthodox Christianity or the *Tewahedo* faith, it is believed the near-sacrifice of Abraham's

---

[53] https://en.wikipedia.org/wiki/Death_and_Resurrection_of_Jesus.
[54] https://en.wikipedia.org/wiki/Lent.
[55] https://en.wikipedia.org/wiki/Good_Friday.
[56] https://en.wikipedia.org/wiki/Paschal_Vigil.

loved son Isaac (Genesis 22), which was a test of faith from God to Abraham, was interrupted by a voice of an angel from the heavens and the sending of a lamb for the sacrifice instead. This Old Testament story is said to be a prophetic foreshadowing[57] of God sending his only beloved Son for the world as a sacrifice and the fulfilling of Abraham's promise.

Easter in Ethiopia, Eritrea, and its Diaspora (Jews dispersed beyond Israel) communities is a day when people celebrate; there is a release of enjoyment after the long buildup of suffering which has taken place to represent Christ's fasting for forty days and forty nights. People often have food, and for most Orthodox Christians locally brewed alcohol from fresh honey (*tej*, *tella*, and *katikala*) while to a certain extent Ethiopian-Eritrean Protestantism generally discourages heavy alcohol.

Ethiopians and Eritreans in the West especially those of the Catholic and Protestant denominations celebrate Easter on both the Eastern and Western days. While most Ethiopian-Eritrean Orthodox Christians in the West refrain from doing so because celebrating the Western Easter celebration would interfere with the Orthodox Eastern fasting season.

Just think, the explosion of Christianity in Africa started in the Old Testament with the visit of Queen Sheba to Israel and in the New Testament with the baptism of the Ethiopian official by the apostle Phillip. The Word of the Lord flourished with help of Ethiopians throughout the Bible.

---

[57] https://en.wikipedia.org/wiki/Typology_(theology).

Chapter 13

Rock-Cut Churches of Lalibela, the Jerusalem of Ethiopia

*[To the Ethiopians of Lalibela:] Listen
to me, you who pursue righteousness
and who seek the LORD: Look to the
rock from which you were cut and to the
quarry from which you were hewn.*
—Isaiah 51:1

The Church of Saint George showing its
base and walls, almost eight stories high

Lalibela is a town in Amhara Region,[58] Ethiopia famous for its rock-cut monolithic churches.[59] The whole of Lalibela is a large antiquity of the medieval and postmedieval civilization of Ethiopia.

Lalibela is one of Ethiopia's holiest cities, second only to Axum, and a center of pilgrimage. Unlike Axum, the population of Lalibela is almost completely Ethiopian Orthodox Christian.

The churches were not constructed in a traditional way but rather were hewn from the living rock of monolithic blocks. These blocks were further chiselled out, forming doors, windows, columns, various floors, roofs, etc.

Carved out of volcanic tuff rock, the famous churches have been built in a variety of styles. Some of them were chiseled into the face of the rock, where others stand as isolated blocks like the iconic church of Saint George constructed in the shape of the cross. A complex and extensive system of drainage ditches, tunnels, and subterranean passageways connects the underground structures. These buildings are different because they were built from the top down everywhere in the world; structures are built from the ground up.

There is nothing comparable in the world. This gigantic work was further completed with an extensive system of drainage ditches, trenches, and ceremonial passages—some with openings to hermit caves and catacombs.

The rock-hewn churches of Lalibela are located in the Western Ethiopian highlands near the town of Lalibela named after the late twelfth and early thirteenth century King Lalibela of the Zagwe dynasty. He commissioned the massive building project of eleven rock-hewn monolithic churches to recreate the holy city of Jerusalem in his own kingdom.

---

[58] https://en.wikipedia.org/wiki/Amhara_Region.
[59] https://en.wikipedia.org/wiki/Monolithic_church.

The site remains in use by the Ethiopian Orthodox Christian Church to this day, and it remains an important place of pilgrimage for Ethiopian Orthodox worshippers.

It cannot be repeated enough that Ethiopia was one of the earliest nations to adopt Christianity in the first half of the fourth century, and its historical roots date to the time of the apostles to the reign of the Zagwe king Gebre Mesqel Lalibela (r. ca. 1181–1221).[60]

The saint-king was named because a swarm of bees is said to have surrounded him at his birth, which his mother took as a sign of his future reign as the emperor of Ethiopia.

The names of several places in the modern town and the general layout of the rock-cut churches themselves are said to mimic names and patterns observed by King Lalibela during the time he spent as a youth in Jerusalem and the holy land.

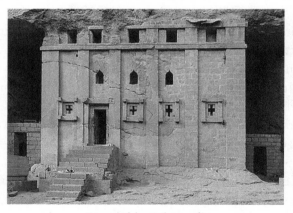

Biete Abba Libanos[61]

Legends claim the churches were built in twenty-four years; however, archaeologists consider this impossible. Even

---

[60] https://en.wikipedia.org/wiki/Gebre_Mesqel_Lalibela.
[61] https://en.wikipedia.org/wiki/File:Bete_Abba_Libanos.jpg.

today, accomplishing this work using carbon steel tipped chisels and diamond blades would be remarkable.

There are also many other peculiarities about its construction, such as the fact that the massive amount of stone and Earth that would have had to be removed around the churches and from their hollowed out interiors was nowhere to be found.

This rural town is known around the world for its churches carved from within the earth from *living rock*, which play an important part in the history of rock-cut architecture. Though the dating of the churches is not well established, most are thought to have been built during the reign of Lalibela, namely during the twelfth and thirteenth centuries.

UNESCO identifies eleven churches assembled in four groups. The rock-hewn churches of Lalibela are located in the Western Ethiopian highlands near the town of Lalibela named after the late twelfth and early thirteenth century.

King Lalibela of the Zagwe dynasty commissioned the massive building project of eleven rock-hewn churches to recreate the holy city of Jerusalem in his own kingdom.

Biete Maryam[62]

---

[62] https://en.wikipedia.org/wiki/File:Bete_Maryam_01.jpg.

The site remains in use by the Ethiopian Orthodox Christian Church to this day, and it remains an important place of pilgrimage for Ethiopian Orthodox worshipeprs.

Lalibela, revered as a saint, is said to have seen Jerusalem and then attempted to build a new Jerusalem as his capital in response to the capture of old Jerusalem by Muslims in 1187. Each church was carved from a single piece of rock to symbolize spirituality and humility.

The churches were not constructed from the ground up but chiselled out of the town's red volcanic rock hills instead. Lalibela monolithic churches plunge 40 to 50 meters into the ground. Legend has it that the thousands of laborers who toiled on Lalibela's new Jerusalem by day were matched by angels who continued the work by night.

All eleven churches are arranged in two groups and are connected with passageways 11 meters (36 feet) deep. The largest church, the House of Medhane, stands at a height of 10 meters (33 feet) and is 33 meters (108 feet) long and 22 meters (72 feet) wide.

The rock-hewn churches of Lalibela were designated one of UNESCO's original twelve world heritage sites in 1978.[63] The list has since grown to over a thousand.

Several of the main churches are sheltered from the elements by rather bulky slabs of UNESCO-supplied metal sheet to prevent erosion. One cannot dispute the necessity of the structures, but they do detract from the majesty of the churches.

---

[63] http://whc.unesco.org/?cid=31&mode=table.

Biete Amanuel[64]

Biete Meskel[65]

---

[64] https://en.wikipedia.org/wiki/File:Bete_Emmanuel.jpg.
[65] https://en.wikipedia.org/wiki/File:Biete_Meskel.jpg.

Biete Medhane Alem over four stories high

The Northern Group

- *Biete Medhane Alem*[66] (House of the Saviour of the World) home to the *Lalibela Cross*
- *Biete Maryam*[67] (House of Miriam/House of Mary) possibly the oldest of the churches and a replica of the tombs of Adam and Christ
- *Biete Golgotha Mikael*[68] (House of Golgotha Mikael) known for its arts and said to contain the tomb of King Lalibela
- *Biete Meskel*[69] (House of the Cross)
- *Biete Denagel*[70] (House of Virgins)

---

[66] https://en.wikipedia.org/wiki/Biete_Medhane_Alem.

[67] https://en.wikipedia.org/wiki/Biete_Maryam.

[68] https://en.wikipedia.org/w/index.php?title=Biete_Golgotha_Mikael&action=edit&redlink=1.

[69] https://en.wikipedia.org/wiki/Biete_Meskel.

[70] https://en.wikipedia.org/w/index.php?title=Biete_Denagel&action=edit&redlink=1.

The Western Group

- *Church of Saint George*[71] thought to be the most finely executed and best preserved church

The Eastern Group

- *Biete Amanuel* (House of Immanuel) possibly the former royal chapel
- *Biete Qeddus Mercoreus* (House of Saint Mercurius/ House of Mark the Evangelist) which may be a former prison
- *Biete Abba Libanos* (House of Abbot Libanos)
- *Biete Gabriel-Rufael* (House of the angels Gabriel and Raphael) possibly a former royal palace linked to a holy bakery
- *Biete Lehem* (Hebrew "Bethlehem" means "House of Bread")

The king of Lalibela set out to build a symbol of the holy land when pilgrimages to it were rendered impossible by the historical situation. In the Church of Biet Golgotha are replicas of the tomb of Christ and of Adam and the crib of the nativity. The holy city of Lalibela became a substitute for the holy places of Jerusalem and Bethlehem and as such has had considerable influence on Ethiopian Christianity.

The whole of Lalibela offers an exceptional testimony to the medieval and postmedieval civilization of Ethiopia, including next to the eleven churches, the extensive remains of traditional two-story circular village houses with interior staircases, and thatched roofs.

---

[71] https://en.wikipedia.org/wiki/Church_of_Saint_George,_Lalibela.

The rock-hewn churches of Lalibela are still preserved in their natural settings. The association of the rock-hewn churches and the traditional vernacular circular houses in the surrounding area still demonstrate evidences of the ancient village layout. The original function of the site as a pilgrimage place still persists and provides evidence of the continuity of social practices. The intangible heritages associated with church practices are still preserved.

Part 10
Lalibela's Water Supply to Each Church and Baptism Pools

An even greater mystery to how the churches were built is the availability of the water supply to each of the eleven churches and their baptism pools.

There was, for example, plenty of water in the valley rivers that flowed hundreds of meters below the hilltop site of Lalibela. But a site by the river would not have been easy to defend, and this reason is often given as an explanation for the choice of the present site atop the plateau.

There was, however, another reason Lalibela picked this spot. Here, remarkably at the very top, there was water, although there are no hydrogeological studies of the site. It is close to indisputable that the water comes from an artesian aquifer—the source of which, as is common for aquifers, is miles away—in this case, in the three-thousand-meter-plus high Last Mountain range to the north.

The tallest mountain of the range is Mt. Abune Yosef some twenty kilometers away, but one three-thousand-meter peak is only three kilometers away. Lalibela, at an elevation of about two thousand meters, is, in essence, in the foothills of these mountains. These springs were certainly known by local villagers long before the village there was transformed into a capital.

But there is a big difference between water leaching out of the rocks and the water distribution system that is in place now. The design of this water distribution system was the work of an expert, who, so it seems, was brought in especially for this purpose. Not much is known about the designer of the artesian aquifer other than his name, Abba Libanos.

He held considerable stature, and there is even a church named after him. Inside the church, one can still see a painting probably a nineteenth century copy of a lost original, which shows Libanos holding a cane against the top of a mountain. The cane with a cross on top though made of wood has a metal tip in the shape of a small spade. From the spot where it touches the earth, there springs a river.

Who Libanos was is open to conjecture. Did he travel to other cities to perfect his craft? Did other water specialists come to Lalibela as part of his team? It is also possible that Libanos was not Ethiopian but came from the Levant and, if so, must certainly have known places like Petra (now in Jordan), which had an extensive and highly ingenious water system that collected water from rain as well as from outlying springs.

Libano, being a Christian, would have most certainly been eager to flee the Islamic invaders who were closing in on the Christian kingdoms of Jerusalem and Tyre during the early thirteenth century. This remarkable design of the artesian water system had to repeat numerous times, since almost all the principal churches have a well or pool associated with them.

In the wet season, these overflow, and most of the water run through specially-constructed channels into the Jordan River.

In most of the square pools, papyrus grows on the surface. These pools serve a special religious rituals still in effect
today. Infertile women during a special ceremony are lowered
into the pool as a way to restore their fecundity. The papyrus, symbolizing rebirth, the birth of Moses, and indeed the
Nile River, adds to the symbolic charge of the pools. Bete
Giyorgis, the famous cross-shaped church, has not only a
pool of its own but also a special east-oriented corridor that
leads to a spring—the overflow from the spring going into a
channel that leads to the Jordan River.

Baptism pool at each of the eleven churches
Scientist questions the origin of the water at a
four-thousand-foot elevation mountain

Chapter 14

Ark of the Covenant—
Home at Mount Zion

"In those days, when your numbers have
increased greatly in the land," declares
the LORD, "people will no longer say,
'The ark of the covenant of the LORD.'
It will never enter their minds or be
remembered; it will not be missed,
nor will another one be made."
—Jeremiah 3:16

> *Then God's temple in heaven was opened,*
> *and within his temple was seen the ark*
> *of his covenant. And there came flashes*
> *of lightning, rumblings, peals of thunder,*
> *an earthquake and a severe hailstorm.*
>
> —Revelation 11:19

The Ark of the Covenant is a chest that held tablets engraved with the Ten Commandments. According to the Hebrew Bible, the ark was constructed by the Israelites while they were camping out in the Sinai desert after they fled Egypt. The ark vanished when the Babylonians conquered Jerusalem in 587 BC.

The ark has a number of seemingly magical powers according to the Hebrew Bible. In one story, the Jordan River stopped flowing and remained still while a group of priests carrying the ark crossed the river. Other stories describe how the Israelites took the ark with them into the battle where the powers of the ark helped the Israelites defeat their enemies.

The relationship between Ethiopia and the Ark of the Covenant can only be hypothesized, although some ancient texts make reference to it.

Through the centuries, Ethiopian Christians had claimed that the ark rests in a chapel in the small town of Axum in their country's northern highlands. It arrived nearly three thousand years ago, they say, and had been guarded by a succession of virgin monks (eunuchs) who, once anointed, were forbidden to set foot outside the chapel grounds until they die.

The story of the Ark of the Covenant is told in the *Kebra Nagast* (Glory of the Kings), Ethiopia's chronicle of its royal line: "The Queen of Sheba, one of its first rulers, traveled to Jerusalem to partake of King Solomon's wisdom; on her way home, she bore Solomon's son, Menelik." Later Menelik went to visit his father, and on his return journey was accompanied by the firstborn sons of some Israelite nobles, who, unbeknown to Menelik, stole the ark and carried it with them to Ethiopia. When Menelik learned of the theft, he reasoned that since the ark's frightful powers hadn't destroyed his retinue, it must be God's will that it remain with him.

The *Kebra Nagast* covers the visit of Queen Sheba to Israel to meet with King Solomon. The Ethiopian Bible, the *Kebra Nagast*, is much older than the Bible.

Many verses in the Bible make reference to gifts that will brought to God at the new Jerusalem. Will the Ark of the Covenant be one of those gifts? It is important enough repeating, "The Ethiopian will bring a gift to God at the new heaven."

> At that time gifts will be brought to the LORD Almighty from a people tall and smooth-skinned, from a people feared far and wide, an aggressive nation of strange speech, whose land is divided by rivers—the gifts will be brought to Mount Zion, the place of the Name of the LORD Almighty. (Isa. 18:7)

It would be farfetched to assume that the gift from the Ethiopia would be the Ark of the Covenant. The question has been raised, "Why were Ethiopians chosen in so many instances to do God's work, which was to spread the good news of the coming of Jesus?" The questions are raised, "What else does Ethiopia or Ethiopian people need to do that is not very clear in the Bible? Is it the return of the Ark of the Covenant?"

Based on the biblical accomplishments by Ethiopians, we cannot dismiss the claim by them that an Ethiopian monk (eunuch) is guarding the Ark of the Covenant.

> For thus saith the LORD unto the eunuchs that keep my sabbaths, and choose the things that please me, and take hold of my covenant even unto them will I give in mine house and within my walls a place and a name better than of sons and of daughters: I will give them an everlasting name, that shall not be cut off. (Isa. 56:4–6)

Some pessimist would say concerning this chapter, "Is it wise to speculate on the location of the Ark of the Covenant?" The answer would be that for the nonbelievers, the ark is safe because they do not believe it's there; and for the believers, they will not go against the will of the Lord, and God will not allow it to happen. Remember the verse:

> "In those days, when your numbers have increased greatly in the land," declares the LORD, "people will no longer say, 'The ark of the covenant of the LORD.' It will never enter their minds or be remembered; it will not be missed, nor will another one be made." (Jer. 3:16)

Sources

Tamrat Taddesse, *Church and State in Ethiopia* (Oxford: Clarendon Press, 1972), p. 61 n.3.

Michael P. Kucher. The Water Supply System of Siena, Italy: The Medieval Roots of the Modern Networked City, (New York: Routledge, 2005).

Wheeler, H. W (1980), *Artesian bores of South Australia : an annotated photographic record,* 1939–1948, Pioneer Books.

Frances Gies and Joseph Gies, *Cathedral, Forge, and Waterwheel* subtitled "Technology and Invention in the Middle Ages". Harper Perennial, 1995, page 112.

Harden, J. M., "An introduction to Ethiopic Christian Literature" (1926) Chapter II, "Brief Historical Sketch of the Country and Church.

Markessini, Joan (2012). Around the World of Orthodox Christianity—Five Hundred Million Strong: The Unifying Aesthetic Beauty. Dorrance Publishing.

Morgan, Giles (2017). St George: The patron saint of England. Oldcastle Books. *E. A. Wallis Budge (1 August 2014). A History of Ethiopia: Volume I: Nubia and Abyssinia. Routledge. p. 7.*

Oliver, Roland (1975). *The Cambridge History of Africa,* Volume 3. Cambridge University Press. p. 106. https://books.google.com/?id=GWjxR61xAe0C&p-g=PA106&dq=death+of+a+local+ruler+badit+ethio-

pia#v=onepage&q=death%20of%20a%20local%20
ruler%20badit%20ethiopia&f=false.

Braukhaper, Ulrich (2002). *Islamic History and Culture in Southern Ethiopia: Collected Essays.* LIT Verlag Münster. p. 21. Retrieved 12 March 2017.

Harold G. Marcus. (1994). *A history of Ethiopia. Berkeley, Calif.:* University of California Press.

Isabel Boavida, Herve Pennec, and Manuel Joao Ramos, eds. *Pedro Paez's History of Ethiopia, 1622.* Vol. 1. Trans. Christopher J. Tribe. London: Hakluyt Society, 2011. p. 80–89.

Robel Arega. "Fasting in the Ethiopian Orthodox Church". Ethiopian Orthodox Tewahedo Church Sunday School Department—Mahibere Kidusan. Why Fifty-Five Days?. Retrieved 30 March 2017.

TrueChristian—As a christian, what is the bible's take on secular music and alcohol?". reddit. Retrieved 2018-06-22.

James Jeffrey (22 March 2017). "Ethiopia: fasting for 55 days" Deufsche Welle. Retrieved 24 March 2017.

25th Dynasty

Broekman, G.P.F. (2015). *The order of succession between Shabaka and Shabataka. A different view on the chronology of the Twenty-fifth Dynasty.* GM 245. p. 29.

Mokhtar, G. (1990). General History of Africa. California, USA: University of California Press. pp. 161–163.

Emberling, Geoff (2011). Nubia: Ancient Kingdoms of Africa. New York: Institute for the Study of the Ancient World. pp. 9–11.

Silverman, David (1997). Ancient Egypt. New York: Oxford University Press. pp. 36–37.

Spread

Johnson, Todd M.; Zurlo, Gina A.; Hickman, Albert W.; Crossing, Peter F. (November 2017). "Christianity 2018: More African Christians and Counting Martyrs". International Bulletin of Mission Research. 42 (1).

Mauro, J.-P. (24 July 2018). "Africa overtakes Latin America for the highest Christian population". *Aleteia—Catholic Spirituality, Lifestyle, World News, and Culture.* Retrieved 24 September 2019.

Ancient African Christianity: An Introduction to a Unique Context and Tradition By David E. Wilhite, page 332-33

Ancient African Christianity: An Introduction to a Unique Context and Tradition By David E. Wilhite, page 336-33

Hrbek, Ivan (1992). Africa from the Seventh to the Eleventh Century. Unesco. International Scientific Committee for the Drafting of a General History of Africa. J. Currey. p. 34.

Kollman, Paul. "Classifying African Christianities: Past, Present, and Future: Part One." Journal of Religion in Africa, vol. 40, no. 1, 2010, pp. 3–32.

Modern Day

Hansberry, William Leo. Pillars in Ethiopian History; the William Leo Hansberry African History Notebook. Washington: Howard University Press, 1974.

Berhanu Abegaz, "Ethiopia: A Model Nation of Minorities" (accessed 6 April 2006).

S. C. Munro-Hay, *Aksum: An African Civilization of Late Antiquity* (Edinburgh: University Press, 1991), p. 77.

Ethiopia: International Religious Freedom Report 2006 U.S. State Department (accessed 6 May 2009).

UNESCO World Heritage Centre. "Rock-Hewn Churches, Lalibela". unesco.or.

Phillipson, David (2009). Ancient Churches of Ethiopia: Fourth-fourteenth Centuries. Yale University Press. p. 179.

Mark Jarzombek, "Lalibela and Libanos: The King and the Hydro-Engineer of 13th Century Ethiopia" (PDF), Construction Ahead, (May–June 2007): 16–2.

The Ezana Stone

The *Ezana Stone* is a stela (ancient world monument) from the ancient Kingdom of Axum believed to have been erected some time during the first half of the fourth century of the current era by King Ezana of Axum in what is now called Ethiopia.

The stone monument documents the conversion of King Ezana to Christianity and his conquest of various neighboring areas, including Meroë. From AD 330 to 356, King Ezana ruled the ancient Kingdom of Axum centered in the Horn of Africa. He fought against the Nubians and commemorated his victories on stone tablets in praise of God.

These liturgical epigraphs were written in various ancient languages, including the Ethiopian Semitic Ge'ez, the South Arabian, Sabaean, and Greek. The king's engravings in stone provided a trilingual monument in different languages similar to the Rosetta Stone.

About the Author

Dr. Lawrence E. Henry received his EdD in counseling/educational psychology from Northern Arizona University, specializing in clinical and psychological assessment. He has over twenty years of experience as a clinical psychologist and performed as the clinical director in the Arizona State correctional facility. He is the author of three books revealing the wonders of God: *In Search of Wisdom: The Pickle Jar Theory, Fruit of the Spirit,* and the *Water Fountain.*

In Search of Wisdom was a lifelong search for scientific knowledge presents the scientific evidence of the truth disclosed in the Bible. In 1983, Dr. Henry cofounded the Full Gospel Church of Arizona, which is a multicultural church in Phoenix, Arizona.

CPSIA information can be obtained
at www.ICGtesting.com
Printed in the USA
LVHW040930101120
671142LV00002B/125